JUV
D
736
.044
1994

$17.95

D0810339

leaders of
...rld War II.

DATE			
2-96			

BAKER & TAYLOR

A M E R I C A N
P R O F I L E S

MILITARY LEADERS OF
WORLD WAR II

.

Walter Oleksy

Facts On File®

AN INFOBASE HOLDINGS COMPANY

To my brother Johnny,
who volunteered for the Navy after just
turning seventeen
and served in the Pacific during the war,

And to my Army buddies
in the Third Armored Division, 1955–1957

Military Leaders of World War II

Copyright © 1994 by Walter Oleksy

All rights reserved. No part of this book may be reproduced or utilized in any form or by any means, electronic or mechanical, including photocopying, recording, or by any information storage or retrieval systems, without permission in writing from the publisher. For information contact:

Facts On File, Inc.
460 Park Avenue South
New York NY 10016

Library of Congress Cataloging-in-Publication Data
Oleksy, Walter G., 1930–
    Military leaders of World War II / Walter Oleksy.
        p. cm.—(American profiles)
    Includes bibliographical references and index.
    ISBN 0-8160-3008-1
    1. World War, 1939–1945—Biography—Juvenile literature.
    2. United States—Armed Forces—Biography—Juvenile literature.
    3. World War, 1939–1945—United States—Juvenile literature.
    4. Soldiers—United States—Biography—Juvenile literature.
    [1. World War, 1939–1945—Biography. 2. United States—Armed Forces—Biography. 3. Soldiers.] I. Title. II. Series: American profiles (Facts on File, Inc.)
    D736.O44 1994
    940.54'4973—dc20   93-33641

Facts On File books are available at special discounts when purchased in bulk quantities for businesses, associations, institutions or sales promotions. Please call our Special Sales Department in New York at 212/683-2244 or 800/322-8755.

Text design by Ron Monteleone
Jacket design by Fred Pusterla
Printed in the United States of America

MP FOF 10 9 8 7 6 5 4 3 2 1

This book is printed on acid-free paper.

Rn 96

Contents

Introduction

World War II (1939–1945) was a global conflict involving every major power in the world. The war had multiple causes. In Europe, economic hardships and political unrest after World War I led to the rise of two aggressive powers. The establishment of Benito Mussolini's Fascist regime in Italy in 1925 and Adolph Hitler's Nazi Germany in 1933 threatened to upset the balance of power in Europe. Also, Japan's desire to expand its territories in the Pacific put that nation on a collision course with the British, French, Dutch, and Americans, all of whom had interests there.

The United States entered World War II on December 8, 1941, the day after the Japanese attacked the American air and naval bases at Pearl Harbor, Hawaii. Japan was an ally of Germany whose armies had already invaded Austria, Poland, France, Yugoslavia, and Czechoslovakia, and whose bombers were raining terror on London, England. A few days after the United States declared war on Japan, Japan's allies, Germany and Italy, declared war on the United States. The United States' major allies became Great Britain, the Free French, China, and the Soviet Union.

America's military leaders decided it would be almost impossible to fight a global war on every front at the same time, so they engaged in a limited war in the Pacific while concentrating on winning the war in Europe.

For the purposes of this book, five leaders were selected from each "theater" of war, though many others could justifiably have been chosen.

One woman, aviatrix Jacqueline Cochran, was selected to represent the enormous contribution of women in the war. While not permitted to serve in combat, thousands of American women played important support and defense roles in the army, navy, and air corps, as well as the various nursing corps. Some American women serving in the war in both the Pacific and Europe nevertheless saw action and were wounded or gave their lives along with the fighting men.

World War II was the greatest war and the largest-scale conflict ever fought. Skilled and courageous officers were needed to sail the ships, fly the planes, and train and lead the soldiers into battle. The United States Army, Navy, and Marines came through with leaders who proved themselves superior in strategy and in battle to those of the enemy.

In the Pacific, some of the outstanding U.S. leaders were Colonel Claire Chennault who organized and led the "Flying Tigers" in air strikes against the Japanese in China; Colonel Evans Carlson, whose "Carlson's Raiders" Marines played a pivotal role in the victories on Makin Island, Guadalcanal, Tarawa, and Saipan; General Douglas MacArthur who was commander of U.S. operations in the Far East and led the force that liberated the Philippines; Admiral Chester Nimitz, commander of the U.S. Pacific Fleet, who was chief strategist for the historically significant battles of the Coral Sea, Midway, and the Solomon Islands; and Admiral William F. "Bull" Halsey, commander of the U.S. Third Fleet, who led the naval task force to victories in the Marshall and Gilbert Islands, Guadalcanal, and at the battle of Leyte Gulf.

In Europe, the outstanding U.S. military leaders included General Dwight D. Eisenhower, commander and chief strategist of the U.S. forces in England and on the continents of Europe and Africa; Jacqueline Cochran, who organized and led the Women's Air Force Service Pilots in flying planes from North America to the European war zone, thus relieving pilots for combat; General Omar Bradley, commander of the U.S. Second Army in victories in Tunisia and Sicily, the Normandy invasion of Europe, and leader of the 12th Army Corps in battles through France and into Germany; Captain Curtis LeMay, the Army Air Corps commander who led the 305th Bombardment Group in air raids over Germany, then commanded the 20th and 21st Bomber Commands in the Pacific, which devastated Tokyo with "fire-raids" shortly before the atomic bombs dropped on Hiroshima and Nagasaki caused the Japanese to surrender on August 14, 1945; and General George S. Patton, perhaps the greatest pure strategist among the Americans, who led the 2nd Armored Division to victories in North Africa, and then commanded the Third Army, which spearheaded armored drives through France and Germany until the Germans surrendered on May 7, 1945.

John Keegan, military historian, wrote in his book *The Second World War,* "The Second World War is the largest single event in human history, fought across six of the world's seven continents and all its oceans. It killed fifty million human beings, left hundreds of millions of others wounded in mind or body and materially devastated much of the heartland of civilization."

In the war in the Pacific, 1.2 million Japanese and 292,000 American servicemen were killed. In Europe, over four million German servicemen died in the war, 3.25 million more died from causes other than combat, and another million were listed as missing. Among the Allies, the United States lost 400,000 men in battle, the British and French each lost about 250,000, and more than six million Soviet soldiers died.

The Second World War was the largest and greatest war ever fought. The survival of freedom-loving nations of the world depended upon their peoples' willingness and ability to fight to preserve or restore their freedom. Most likely, the war would not have been won by the Allies without the help of American GIs and their leaders. Perhaps the greatest of the American military leaders of World War II are represented in this book, a remarkable team that seemed destined to lead the crusade to save the world for democracy.

Colonel Claire Lee Chennault (1890–1958) Leader of the "Flying Tigers"

Maj. Gen. Claire Chennault, leader of the "Flying Tigers."
(Smithsonian Institution)

Claire Chennault organized an ace group of volunteer American fighter pilots who risked their lives in China before the United States and Japan were at war. His "Flying Tigers" made military history even before the war officially started for the United States. They then struck one of the first blows against Japan after its attack on Pearl Harbor on December 7, 1941.

1

Though his unit was disbanded a few months after the start of the war, Chennault and some of his pilots fought on in the Army Air Corps and took part in major victories against the Japanese in China.

Claire Lee Chennault was born on September 6, 1890, in Commerce, Texas, the son of a cotton planter, and grew up in Louisiana. After starting to prepare for a career in scientific agriculture at Louisiana State University, he gave it up to study to become a teacher. By the time World War I began, he was working as principal of a Texas high school.

Chennault put teaching aside and joined the army in November 1917. He was commissioned a 1st lieutenant in the Infantry Reserve, but soon transferred to the aviation section of the Signal Reserve Corps, a communications unit of the army. He was stationed at various fields in the United States during the war and afterward joined the army's air service.

In 1923 he began a three-year assignment in Hawaii as commander of the 19th Pursuit Squadron and began studying aerial tactics. By night he calculated and plotted flight strategy, and by day he test-flew planes in the intricate patterns he planned on paper. During these experiments he came up with the idea of having pieces of artillery attached to parachutes and dropped from planes. This would get antiaircraft, antitank, and other guns down to fighting men on the ground quickly and safely.

Chennault spent the next few years as a flight instructor at various army air fields and was considered one of the outstanding authorities on pursuit aviation, a fearless pilot, and an able leader.

In 1932 he became the leader of a special army flying act known as "Three Men on a Flying Trapeze," putting on probably the dizziest air show ever seen, and at the same time he demonstrated the maneuverability of airplanes under highly expert control. Behind every dip and loop of his air circus, Chennault had carefully worked out calculations of stress and strain on the planes he and two others flew at air races in 1935 and 1936.

Chennault became partly deaf from flying in open planes, but nonetheless rose to the rank of captain in 1929, and major in 1936. He retired from the army the following year, and settled down with his wife and children in a cottage on Lake St. John near Waterproof, Louisiana.

His retirement didn't last long. Two of his flying circus comrades, J.H. Williamson and W.C. McDonald, had gone to China to organize an aviation school sponsored by Madame Chiang Kai-shek, wife of the Nationalist leader who opposed the expansion of communism in China. Chennault's friends urged him to join them, and when the Chinese offered him the position of air adviser, he went to China in July 1937 to take on the job of creating an air force to combat the Japanese, who would launch a full-scale invasion that year.

Chennault, then 47 years old, arrived in China to discover there were less than 100 first-line combat planes in the whole country and that Chinese pilots were insufficiently trained for combat. He realized that, unless the Chinese pilots were better trained, their already insufficient number would diminish quickly.

A few weeks after Chennault began his work in China, the Sino-Japanese War broke out. To solve the problem of how to bolster China's air power, Chennault formed the Chinese National Aviation Commission and set about making the Chinese Air Force into an effective fighting unit. He revised training procedures, taught new tactics, and established a vast radio and telephone network to signal the approach of Japanese bombers.

Chennault taught the Chinese fliers never to fly alone, to make their ammunition count, to strike hard and then head for home. Perhaps most importantly, he taught them to try to out-think the enemy pilots by anticipating the enemy's movements in the air. Chennault himself studied the reactions of Japanese pilots until he was able to tell in advance every move an attacking Japanese squadron would make. He could look through a pair of field glasses and describe to an openmouthed audience of staff officers each detailed move that an attacking Japanese squadron would make before it actually made those moves.

Chennault also put what he learned into practice by flying in combat with Chinese air forces over Shanghai, Nanking, and Chunking, fighting the Japanese. At the same time he was training the Chinese to fight in the air, Chennault set up a series of air bases throughout the interior of China. He also helped organize an air raid system considered to be one of the best in the world.

After three years of training for offense and defense, Chennault stated boldly that, with only a small air force ready to fly with the tactics he had developed, he could flank and destroy any Japanese attempt to invade the South Pacific. He was sure his strategy would work, but needed that air force to carry it out.

Chennault returned to the United States in 1940 to ask the government for planes to help the Chinese defend themselves. He was given about 100 small fighter planes, as well as several bombers, but when he returned to China and the planes arrived there, he found a shortage of replacement parts so severe that half the planes had to be kept in shop in order to keep the others in the air. There also weren't enough skilled mechanics or enough ammunition and, worst of all, not enough pilots.

Chennault returned to the United States in the summer of 1941 and asked Army Air Corps officials to give him some volunteers to both repair and fly the planes in China. Not wanting to get that politically involved in China's war with Japan, the U.S. government gave him permission only to recruit the personnel he needed.

Chennault criss-crossed the country, going to air bases and talking to ex-army, navy, and Marine pilots and mechanics about the desperate need for them in China. The Chinese authorized him to offer pilots a salary of $600 to $750 a month plus a $500 bounty for every Japanese plane they shot down.

After a few months, Chennault had 112 volunteers, most of whom were eager to see action and didn't even ask about pay.

He took the volunteers to Burma, just south and west of China, and set up a base camp 150 miles above Rangoon, the capital city of Burma, off the Bay of Bengal. Burma had separated from nearby British India a few years before and enjoyed a kind of independence, but was of great strategic importance to both China and Japan and soon would be invaded by the Japanese.

In Burma, Chennault proceeded to create the American Volunteer Group (the AVG) the way a coach would create a great football team. He also systematically studied the P-40 fighters at his command and soon realized that most of his pilots were leery about the planes, which were considered obsolete and dangerous to fly. Back in the United States, P-40s were called "pilot-killers" and were said to be hard to handle at low speeds. To make matters worse, almost none of Chennault's new pilots had ever flown one.

Chennault analyzed the capabilities of the enemy's Zero fighter and found the P-40 superior in several categories that could make it a better plane in aerial combat. While two slabs of armorplate made the plane extremely heavy, they also protected the pilot's back and head from the rear. It carried six machine guns: two heavy .50-caliber machine guns mounted on the front of the fuselage and synchronized to fire through the whirling propeller, and four .30-caliber machine guns mounted in the wings. All were sighted to converge their fire at 250 yards. It was a lot of firepower compared to the Japanese planes, which had much lighter machine guns and therefore less firing range. One of the P-40's chief advantages was that its heavier weight gave it an incredible diving speed in excess of 500 m.p.h., making it easy for the pilots to dive away from pursuing Japanese aircraft.

Chennault concentrated on the P-40's advantages and told his pilots:

> *You must use the strong points of your equipment against the weak points of the enemy. The pilot who can turn his advantage*

against the enemy's weakness will win every time. You can count on a higher top speed, faster dive, and superior firepower. The Jap fighters have a higher rate of climb, higher ceiling, and better maneuverability. They can turn on a dime and climb almost straight up. If they get you into a turning combat they're deadly. Use your speed and driving power to make a pass, shoot, and break away. [Samson, p. xx]

After drilling the pilots on aerial tactics, Chennault had them practice eight hours a day on each maneuver until it was perfect. Then he teamed them in pairs and had them perform the maneuvers until they could do them perfectly in formation. By November 1941 he had ready two fully trained squadrons of 18 men each and a partial squadron of eight. Meanwhile, air bases, repair shops, and shelters had been built.

The P-40s were plain olive-drab fighter planes with few distinguishing characteristics. Some of the pilots had seen a picture in a magazine that showed a P-40 in North Africa that had been painted with sharks' teeth. One evening they asked Chennault if they could paint leering sharks' mouths on the noses of their planes, to make the P-40s look distinctive and more ferocious. Chennault thought that the idea would be good for morale, and that the sharks'-teeth images also might frighten the Japanese pilots, so he consented. Mechanics then painted a leering tiger shark grin, complete with an ominous or sinister eye, on each plane.

As the pilots began flying the newly decorated planes, the Chinese called them "Flying Tiger Sharks," but to the rest of the world they became known as "Flying Tigers." As China's war with Japan spread throughout the fall and winter of 1941, Chennault's volunteers were credited with being the sparkplug of Allied resistance all over the Asiatic mainland.

The Flying Tigers grew into a fighting outfit that for democratic spirit and complete lack of operations formalities may never be equaled, nor would their record of performance soon be equaled.

A few weeks after the attack on Hawaii on December 7, 1941, Japanese planes struck at the Kunming terminal of the Burma

Road, a strategic supply road, but were surprised by the Flying Tigers. On Christmas Eve, Japanese bombers attacked Rangoon a thousand miles away, but Chennault's second squadron intercepted them before they reached the city. Nine Japanese planes were destroyed. The following day, 70 enemy bombers attacked, trying to destroy the Rangoon docks, but the Flying Tigers brought many of them down. Outnumbered 20 to one, with only enough ammunition to fire one minute each time they took to the air, and with no reserves or support, Chennault's pilots kept up the attack for 90 days and destroyed 20 Japanese planes for every one of their own shot down. Ninety-two Japanese pilots were killed for every Flying Tiger lost.

Despite losses of planes and pilots, and a shortage of repair parts and ammunition, the Flying Tigers held the skies over Burma for the Allies throughout February 1942. The rest of the world marveled at the heroics of a few American volunteers flying side-by-side with Britain's Royal Air Force, winning victory after victory.

In May 1942, Chennault said if he had 2,000 planes he could wipe out the Japanese Air Force. Even without them, his Flying Tigers shot down 199 Japanese planes in seven months and 153 more probably destroyed on the ground. Only four of Chennault's pilots and one crew chief had been killed in action, and nine fliers had died in accidents, while 12 P-40s had been shot down in air combat and 61 were destroyed on the ground.

Though the Flying Tigers had caught the imagination of the world, they were soon to be disbanded. They were a winning team, but they were an unorthodox fighting outfit, and U.S. military leaders decided Chennault and his pilots should join the army or go back home. Washington officials thought the higher pay the volunteers were getting from the Chinese was bad for the morale of regular army pilots—and that Chennault's technique of destroying the Japanese was too successful to be used in just three squadrons. He and his men were needed in the regular Army Air Corps to teach other pilots how to win air battles against the enemy.

Chiang Kai-shek had made Chennault a brigadier general in the summer of 1941 and had awarded him the Chinese Military Medal. The following April, he was called to active duty in the U.S. Army and was given the temporary rank of colonel, with permission to continue his activities and relationship with the Chinese government. Five days later he was promoted to brigadier general, and from July 4, 1942, he served with the U.S. Army directly, his group to be replaced by regular Army Air Force pilots.

Chennault made no secret that he regretted the end of the Flying Tigers, especially after only six of his pilots followed him into Army squadrons and most of the ground crews left. But in seven months of daring, ragtag, rear-guard air battles over China, Thailand, and French Indochina, they had made history.

"It was the greatest opportunity an air force commander ever had to get together and train under complete freedom of action a group of fighting men," said Chennault (see Samson). That October, the British honored Chennault for his gallantry during operations in Burma.

Assigned to General Joseph W. Stilwell's command, Chennault put together an Army Air Force offensive capability that he said would expand until Japanese air power everywhere was smashed. His U.S. 14th Air Force pilots raided Japanese bases and planes at Hankow and Canton in South China and gained more fame.

In November 1942, Chennault announced by radio from "Somewhere in Southern China" that he was building up an airport close to Japan as an American "springboard." Now that the Second Front had been opened, he intended to step up the action. The following month it was reported in U.S. newspapers that Chennault's fighters and bombers had been consistently outfighting the Japanese.

Chennault did little flying himself after organizing the Flying Tigers, but worked from morning to night on plans and tactics and on mapping out attacks. While his pilots were in the skies, he was reported to be tense and high-strung. He would pace the floor of his office, leaving behind a swirl of smoke, tramping over a carpet of cigarette ends. He cursed interruptions, and no one could get more than a bark out of him until the last man was safely on the ground or accounted for. When one of his pilots failed to return, Chennault was as hard hit as though the loss were his own son.

While on duty he was a stern disciplinarian, Chennault was said to have "a heart as big as all China," and his men knew it. He insisted on physical fitness for himself and others and played a hard, fast game of tennis whenever he could, pitched like a pro in baseball, and was a whiz at cribbage. Only five feet ten inches tall, his lean, wiry frame gave the impression of being taller. One of his pilots said he would sooner fight under Chennault than anyone in the world. Another called him "one of the hottest acrobatic air pilots ever to kick around an Air Corps pursuit ship."

Chennault headed the U.S. air task force in China until his retirement in August 1945 as a major general. He left shortly before the atomic bombs were dropped on Hiroshima and Nagasaki and the war in the Pacific ended. He retired out of exhaustion and also frustration, because of disagreements with superior officers on how the war could be ended.

Chennault was awarded the Distinguished Service Medal "for outstanding service as an intrepid and effective air commander of the 14th Air Force. Although limited by the difficulties of supply, to the smallest air force in the United States Army, he exacted a heavy toll of enemy personnel, shipping, material and equipment. His force contributed beyond expectation to limiting Japanese air and ground activity and was a major factor in rendering impotent the enemy's air drive in China. In the performance of his task, General Chennault evidenced tactical and strategic skill, foresight and professional attainments which reflect great honor upon himself and the military service."

Chennault went home to Waterproof, Louisiana, and rejoined his wife and children. Restless in retirement, in October 1946 he returned to China, which was then engaged in a protracted civil war between the Nationalists and communists. He formed the Civil Air Transport (CAT), an airline that distributed relief supplies throughout China in aid of the Nationalists. Many of his pilots and ground crew had been members of the Flying Tigers and the 14th Air Force. This work continued until late in 1949 when Chiang Kai-shek evacuated the Nationalist Chinese government from the mainland to Taiwan.

In 1954 Chennault's CAT became involved in the war in Indochina, aiding the French against the Vietnamese communists. The CAT carried tons of supplies to Korea, which greatly helped America in the Korean War. It also flew out thousands of wounded and provided air transportation for U.S. Central Intelligence Agency operatives to establish training bases throughout the Far East.

Chennault returned to Louisiana and, after a long fight with lung cancer, died on July 27, 1958, at Walter Reed Army

Maj. Gen. Claire Chennault (right), head of U.S. air task force in China in 1945, plans aerial strategy with Maj. Gen. Clayton Bissell.
(Courtesy National Air and Space Museum, Smithsonian Institution)

Hospital in Washington, D.C. at the age of 67. Two days before, President Dwight D. Eisenhower phoned to say he had just promoted him to lieutenant general.

Lake Charles Air Force Base in Louisiana was renamed Chennault Air Force Base and, in Taipei, Taiwan, a life-sized bust of Chennault was unveiled in the square near the Capitol building, the first statue of a foreigner ever erected by the Chinese on their own soil.

Chronology

September 6, 1890	born in Commerce, Texas
1917	becomes 1st lieutenant in Infantry Reserve; transfers to aviation section of Signal Corps Reserve
1923	becomes commander of 19th Pursuit Squadron in Hawaii
1926	becomes expert flight instructor
1932	leads flying act, "Three Men on a Trapeze"
1935–36	performs aerial acts in air shows
1937	retires from air force; goes to China to create an air force for Chiang Kai-shek
1941	forms "Flying Tigers"; plans strategy for air resistance against Japanese
1942	called to active duty in Army Air Force, with rank of colonel
1945	retires as major general
1946–49	returns to China; forms Civil Air Transport airline to supply Chinese Nationalists
1954	his CAT supplies French in Indochina
July 27, 1958	promoted to lieutenant general; dies of lung cancer

Further Reading

Book by Claire Chennault
Way of a Fighter: The Memoirs of Claire Lee Chennault. New York: Putnam, 1949.

Books About Claire Chennault
Ford, Daniel. *Flying Tigers.* Washington, D.C.: Smithsonian Institution Press, 1991. Exciting account of Chennault and the American Volunteer Group before and during World War II.

Samson, Jack. *Chennault.* Garden City, N.Y.: Doubleday, 1987. Biography by a former member of Chennault's 14th Air Force in China.

Schultz, Duane. *The Maverick War: Chennault and the Flying Tigers.* New York: St. Martin's Press, 1987. Perhaps the best book on Chennault and the Flying Tigers for young adult readers.

Article About Claire Chennault
Current Biography, 1942. New York: H.W. Wilson, 1942. Summary of his years with the Flying Tigers and his World War II service up to 1942.

Lieutenant Colonel Evans Carlson (1896–1947) Leader of "Carlson's Raiders"

Lt. Col. Evans F. Carlson, USMC, aboard U.S.S. Nautilus on August 18, 1942, just after returning from Makin Island.
(National Archives)

On August 9, 1942, 221 United States Marines of the Second Raider Battalion left Pearl Harbor, Hawaii, aboard two submarines, the *Argonaut* and *Nautilus*. They were about to attempt a surprise hit-and-run attack on Makin atoll in the

Gilbert Islands. It was to be the first raid by Americans against Japanese-held territory in World War II. Their commander was Evans Carlson, son of a Connecticut Congregationalist minister, and their executive officer, James Roosevelt, the son of the president of the United States.

Eight days later, at dawn, they surprised the enemy by landing on a beach the Japanese thought was physically impossible to reach by sea. Without air cover, the Marines suffered heavy losses, as Japanese planes bombed them for over an hour in one intensive strike. But in the 40 hours of fighting that followed, the Marines killed the entire enemy garrison of 300, destroyed two small transport ships, two radio stations, two seaplanes, set 1,000 barrels of aviation gasoline aflame, and burned and leveled all of the enemy's operating military installations. Thirty Marines were killed in the battle.

The Marine victory made front-page headlines back in the United States, where Americans were eagerly waiting for revenge on the Japanese for their surprise attack on Pearl Harbor about nine months earlier. Carlson and his Marine "Raiders" became instant heroes of the war in the Pacific. The *New York Times* devoted a page and a half to the news and ended its account with a stanza of the Raiders' own fighting song, "Carlson's Raiders:"

> *They will sing of the sailor and soldier I know*
> *And tell of the deeds that were done,*
> *But Carlson's Raiders will sing for themselves*
> *And know how the battle was won.*

A *New York Herald-Tribune* editorial praised Carlson by proclaiming, "those who knew him well will readily understand why he was chosen to lead the landing on Makin, why he did such a thorough job and why the Marines sing about him."

Just who was Evans Carlson? The short answer is that he was the leader of the most effective American guerrilla unit in the entire war.

Evans Fordyce Carlson's grandfather had come to this country from Norway in the 1800s, and his father Thomas was born and grew up in a small mining town in the Sierra Mountains of California. Thomas Carlson later graduated from a small theological seminary in New York and became a Congregationalist minister in various small towns in New England. His son Evans was born in Sidney, New York, on February 26, 1896. Evans' mother, Joetta, was descended from Captain Jack Evans who had served on General George Washington's staff during the Revolutionary War.

When Evans was 14, he left home to work on a farm in Vermont. Not very interested in books, the following year he left school to work on the railroads. He became an assistant freight master in New Haven, Connecticut, then worked on a survey crew in New Jersey.

Carlson enlisted in the army when he was 16, giving his age as 22. His parents consented because they thought military service might be the "school" he needed. With minor interruptions for work in civilian jobs, the rest of his career was spent in the armed forces.

After three years of service in the Philippines and the Hawaiian Islands, Carlson decided to leave the army. He was discharged in 1915 with a "high commendation" and the rank of master sergeant. The following year, he was working at welldigging and surveying in California and living in Perris, a small town in the San Gabriel Mountains near San Bernardino. There he became engaged to his landlord's daughter, Dorothy Seccombe. He had become a member of the Army Reserve and was called back into active service as the United States prepared to enter World War I. After he and Miss Seccombe were married in May 1916, he reported for duty at San Diego.

According to Carlson's biographer, Michael Blankfort,

He was unhappy about going back to the army. Marriage had brought him contentment and the hopes of a home. But as long as he had to go back, perhaps something might turn up in the army that would be what he wanted, something that would make him say: Yes, this is it! This is what I am going to do with my life!

During World War I, Carlson became an artillery instructor at Camp Fort Bliss in El Paso, Texas. Overseas, he served as a second lieutenant in France, mostly in administrative work, but during action with the field artillery, he was injured by German gunfire. His service won him citations from the American, French, and Italian governments.

When the war ended, Carlson found he was not at peace with himself. He felt he had not seen enough combat, and was not sure if he should remain in the army and make military service his career. He returned to California and decided a captain's pay would help him to support his wife and their infant son, Evans Jr., but the thought of a safe and secure life in the peacetime army conflicted with his need for adventure. In the army, he sometimes had difficulty obeying the orders of superior officers because of his strong independent streak. As Blankfort put it, "The prospect of being tamed, of not having genuine responsibilities, caught in the craw of his ambition."

Carlson chose to resign from the army, and took a job as a salesman for a California canning company. But the work did not satisfy his need for a meaningful career, and his unhappiness led to a divorce from his wife in 1920. Several years of loneliness and despair followed. In 1922, he decided that the discipline of military life could help him, so he enlisted in the Marines as a private and served both in the United States and Cuba. While he was on duty in Puerto Rico, he met Etelle Sawyer, a U.S. citizen teaching school there. They married in 1924.

From 1927 to 1929, Carlson served in China. As operations and intelligence officer in Shanghai, he was awarded a Marine Corps medal for his service overseas. After helping organize the National Guard in Nicaragua, he returned to Shanghai as intelligence officer of the 4th Marines. From 1933 to 1935 Carlson was post adjutant of the Marine Detachment at Peiping, China. Following two years of duty back in the United States, he returned to Peiping as assistant naval attache and to study Chinese.

In 1937, promoted to captain, Carlson became an observer with the Chinese Communist 8th Route Army, which was fighting the Japanese who had invaded China. He accompanied the unit on a 2,000 mile journey on foot through the remote interior of China, where communist guerrillas were fighting the Japanese. As the first American officer to accompany a Chinese force in a campaign, his job was to study the Chinese pattern of resistance to the Japanese soldiers. As a result, Carlson became an expert on Asian warfare.

After this tour of duty in 1939, Carlson was criticized for saying the Red Chinese soldiers were doing a good job of fighting the Japanese. The U.S. government did not want to take sides in the Chinese Civil War. In a dispute with U.S. Navy officials over his remarks, he resigned his commission and returned to the United States, where he lectured and wrote articles on his experiences in China and warned of the danger of Japanese expansion in the Far East.

In a controversial book, *Twin Stars of China*, Carlson said the communist Chinese had the confidence of the people of China, unlike the Nationalist Chinese leader, Chiang Kai-shek, whom the United States was supporting.

Carlson returned to China in 1940 as a civilian, to study China's capability of resisting the Japanese. On his way back to the United States early the next year, he stopped in Manila to warn General Douglas MacArthur that the Japanese would probably soon attack there. He suggested that the mountains of Luzon, largest island in the Philippines, be made ready for guerrilla fighting, but this was not done.

Convinced war in the Pacific was coming, in April 1941 Carlson conceived the idea of an American guerrilla unit. He was commissioned a major in the Marine Corps Reserve on April 28, and began organizing a raider unit. Two battalions were formed, the 2d Marine Raiders Battalion under Carlson, and another under Col. Merritt A. Edison. Training began in earnest at Camp Elliott in San Diego early in 1942, shortly after the Japanese attacked Pearl Harbor. There Carlson was reunited with his son, who had by then become a captain in the

Marine Corps. Later the Raiders would make practice landings at San Clemente Island off Southern California, and then on Barber's Point off Oahu, Hawaii.

"Carlson's Raiders," as his men came to be known, were all handpicked. Officers were Marine Corps officers, most of them specially selected for their spirit, initiative, and democratic outlook. Most had been outdoorsmen before the war.

Before making his final selection of Raiders, Carlson told each man they would be expected to endure the hardships, dangers, and brutality that guerrilla warfare involved in fighting the Japanese. They would be trained to live off the land, find their own food when necessary, and put up with jungle heat and insects. They also had to be prepared to fight the enemy without mercy and in hand-to-hand combat. That was how the enemy fought. If the candidates still wanted to be Raiders, Carlson took them, but his standards were so high, he rejected six applicants for every man he accepted.

In training, the Raiders usually marched 40 miles a day with full equipment. They soon became skilled in fighting, and expert swimmers and woodsmen. They carried automatic rifles and submachine guns in addition to semi-automatic M-1 Garand rifles, the standard World War II infantry weapon, as well as pistols and knives.

Discipline was important to Carlson, but not the privileges of rank. Running his unit democratically, he abolished officers' privileges and mess, so everyone regardless of rank wore the same clothes, carried the same equipment, and lived alike.

Carlson's biographer says that early in their training as Raiders, they heard their "Old Man" say over and over again, "Training and Gung Ho is everything." They soon learned what he meant.

During Carlson's years in China, he had heard soldiers use the phrase *Kung-ho*, which means "work together." It became Carlson's motto, and he called his unit the Kung-ho Battalion rather than Carlson's Raiders. His men, Americanizing the motto into "Gung Ho!" used it as their battle cry.

Carlson followed his own Gung Ho policy by inviting his men to offer their ideas and feelings in meetings he held to solve problems. He invited open discussion about strategy or other matters, and after each battle invited criticism.

According to Michael Blankfort, Carlson knew when the final test of Gung Ho would come:

> *It would have to come in battle when with every consideration but life and death dissolved out of his men, their natural urge to co-operate would find a reservoir of specific experiences to draw upon. These talks at camp, these examples, these ceaseless reiterations of principles [Carlson often spoke of the need for courage, bravery, and devotion to the cause of freedom] would be, with their training in arms, a pattern transfer on their hearts and minds. Battle would be the hot iron.*

After Pearl Harbor, America badly needed a victory in the Pacific. Carlson and two of his Raider companies, A and B, got one. On August 9, 1942, they set off in two submarines to raid Makin atoll, a tiny island in the Gilberts, near the Equator and about halfway between Hawaii and Australia. Thirteen officers and 208 enlisted men were in the raiding party. The goal was to destroy Japanese naval and air installations, gain information, and divert enemy attention from Marines landing on Guadalcanal, the largest of the Solomon Islands to the east and close to New Guinea and Australia.

Arriving off Makin by submarine, Carlson and his men crowded into 18 small boats. After two hours in stormy seas, they reached the shore. Always the first man ashore and the last to leave, Carlson landed with his Raiders on August 17. But in wading ashore in the rough water, he had hit his right cheekbone, near the eye, against the butt of his rifle. During the ensuing battle, half his face was swollen as if with mumps.

The Japanese were caught by surprise, but within minutes were able to strike the invading party with heavy small-arms fire. Some natives of the Gilbert Islands joined Carlson and gave him details of Japanese strength, which he then radioed to the submarines. They surfaced and fired their six-inch guns at wharfs and other locations where the Japanese were gathered in numbers or at important sites such as ammunition dumps and other supply stores.

Over the next two days, without air cover, the Raiders found themselves under repeated enemy air raids and heavy gunfire from Japanese soldiers on the island. Despite being outnumbered, Carlson and his Raiders outfought the Japanese and were victorious, largely through their belief in and practice of "Gung Ho" unity and philosophy. One of his men, Captain Garrett Graham, is quoted by Blankfort as having said after the raid, "A harmony of spirit and self-sacrifice reigned throughout the expedition. This unity of mind and effort brought success."

Carlson and the Raiders then took part in the battle to reclaim Guadalcanal from the Japanese. U.S. forces had been fighting on Guadalcanal for three months when Carlson's Raiders landed behind the Japanese positions on November 4 to assist regular Marine units. The battle to reclaim Guadalcanal ended on February 2, 1943. The American victory gave the Japanese Army its first major land defeat of the war, prevented it from using the island as an air base in the South Pacific Ocean, and was a great psychological and strategic success for the Americans and their allies.

After Guadalcanal had been retaken from the Japanese, Carlson was awarded the Navy Cross and given a citation for heroism and leadership.

Major General Alexander A. Vandergrift, commander of the 1st Marine Division, cited the Raiders as follows:

For a period of thirty days this battalion [a ground force unit composed of a headquarters and two or more companies], moving through difficult terrain, pursued, harried and, by repeated attacks, destroyed an enemy force of equal or greater size and drove the remnants from the area of operations. During this period the battalion, as a whole or by detachments, attacked the enemy whenever and wherever he could be found in a repeated series of carefully planned and well-executed surprise attacks.

Carlson spoke to his men after the action on Guadalcanal had subsided, telling them, as Blankfort records:

The war is not yet won; the enemy is still strong; there are incontrovertible signs that he realizes he has met his match, but

Admiral Chester W. Nimitz presents the Guadalcanal Medal to Lt. Col. Evans F. Carlson of the 2nd Marine Raiders, on January 1, 1943.
(U.S. Naval Historical Center)

his power still has to be utterly crushed before we can count our job done and our institutions secure. Our course is clear. It is for us at this moment with the memory of the sacrifices of our brothers still fresh, to dedicate again our hearts, our minds and our bodies to the great task that lies ahead. The future of America—yes, the future of the condition of all peoples, rests in our hands . . . Any resolution less than this will spell betrayal of the faith which these staunch comrades reposed in us. God bless you.

Guadalcanal was the end of Carlson's and the Raiders' careers together. The Raiders were sent farther south to the New Hebrides and later to New Zealand and New Caledonia. But Carlson and his men were too independent and unorthodox for the military establishment, so the 2nd Raider Battalion was consolidated with three other battalions into the Marine Raider Regiment, and Carlson was reduced to second in command. His Gung Ho system was discarded.

Ill with malaria, Carlson was sent home to Plymouth, Connecticut, for hospitalization. While recovering, he served as official adviser on a Hollywood motion picture about his Raiders on Makin Island, which was called—appropriately enough—*Gung Ho.*

Returning to active duty in the fall of 1943, Carlson held a staff job at a base in the United States, then was shipped back out to the fighting front in the Pacific. That November he took part in an assault on Tarawa in the Gilbert and Ellice Islands.

"Guadalcanal was something but I never saw anything like this," Carlson told Blankfort of the bloody and bitter Tarawa battle.

Out of about 3,000 Marines who took part in the initial assault at Tarawa, only a few hundred escaped death or injury. Carlson himself landed on the beach 30 minutes after the first wave, under heavy mortar and machine-gun fire.

Carlson, who had been wounded in the chest, later said: "If ever blood and guts were shown, it was right there on the part of the Marine division which did the job. The Japanese had more troops than we did. It was the toughest job the Marines ever had in their 168 years" (Blankfort).

The following year, Carlson was part of the U.S. campaign on Saipan, an island in the Marianas where the Japanese held a strategic air base. He was wounded again, this time while rescuing a wounded enlisted man from a frontline observation post. The island was captured and became a base for American air attacks on the Japanese mainland.

For his service on Saipan, Carlson won the Legion of Merit, a high U.S. Navy decoration, in 1944. His citation, from James Forrestal, secretary of the navy, honored him as an indomitable fighter and a brilliant tactician, and commended him for heroism.

Carlson was promoted to brigadier general and retired from service on July 1 with a medical disability. He became co-chairman of the Committee to Win the Peace and national vice chairman of the Progressive Citizens of America.

Divorced in 1942 from his second wife, Carlson married Peggy Tatum Wayne in 1944 and she had a son, Tony, by a previous marriage. They moved to Brightwood, a little town on the Oregon coast near fruit and dairy farms. He intended to run for the United States Senate but was stricken with a serious heart ailment and did not enter the race. He died of a heart attack shortly afterward, at the age of 51, in Portland, on May 27, 1947.

Chronology

February 26, 1896	born in Sidney, New York
1912	joins U.S. Army at age 16
1915	discharged from army
1916	serves in Mexican expedition
1917	marries; rejoins army and serves in France
1918–21	returns to civilian life
1922	joins Marines and serves in Cuba
1927–29	serves in Shanghai, China
1933–35	assistant naval attache in Peiping, China
1937–39	promoted to captain; observes guerrilla tactics of Chinese Communist 8th Route Army
1939	resigns and writes books about Chinese Army
1940	returns to China as civilian; studies country's ability to resist Japanese invasion
1941	rejoins Marines; forms guerrilla unit, "Carlson's Raiders"
1942	leads Raiders to victories on Makin Island and Guadalcanal
1943	wounded in Marine assault on Tarawa
1944	wounded again in Saipan campaign; awarded Legion of Merit; retires
May 27, 1947	dies in Portland, Oregon

Further Reading

Book by Evans Carlson
Twin Stars of China. New York: Dodd, Mead, 1940. Carlson's observations of China and its defensive capabilities.

Book About Evans Carlson
Blankfort, Michael. *The Big Yankee, The Life of Carlson of the Raiders.* Boston: Little, Brown, 1947. Only complete biography of Carlson, by a personal friend.

Article About Evans Carlson
Current Biography, 1943. New York: H.W. Wilson, 1943. Biography of Carlson up to 1943.

General Douglas MacArthur (1880–1964) U.S. Far East Commander

General Douglas MacArthur.
(U.S. Army Military History Institute)

Douglas MacArthur was born January 26, 1880, at Fort Dodge, an army post that is now part of Little Rock, Arkansas. It was here that he got his first taste of battle when he was four years old. His father, Brigadier General Arthur MacArthur, a veteran of the Civil War, was commanding another army outpost, Fort Selden near El Paso, Texas, when Indians attacked. Douglas left the family's home in the fort to see what all the commotion was about, and his mother took him back inside just as arrows began to fly.

Douglas MacArthur grew up wanting to continue in the family tradition of serving in the military. He went to schools on military posts and won an appointment to West Point in 1899. A gifted student, he graduated in 1903 at the top of his class of 93 cadets. His grade-point average of 98.14 was never equaled during his military career of more than half a century.

MacArthur served in the Philippines and in Japan, and in 1906 began a year's service as aide to his father's friend, President Theodore Roosevelt. He then studied engineering and was assigned to duty stations in Kansas, Texas, and the Panama Canal Zone. He was attached to the army general staff in 1913 and three years later scouted Mexican positions during the U.S.'s "punitive expedition" against the bandit chief Pancho Villa.

At the outbreak of World War I, the 37-year-old MacArthur, then a major in the Engineer Corps, served as chief of staff of the 42nd Division, under Major General Charles T. Menoher, when it went to France in October 1917.

In June 1918, MacArthur was given command of the 84th Infantry Brigade, which he led into battle that September in the St. Mihiel offensive in northeast France. It was the first battle of the war in which American forces fought independently of the other allies, and was a major victory. He repeated the success in the Meuse-Argonne campaign in November 1918 in the same region, another allied victory carried by Americans.

MacArthur was an exceptionally brave soldier. He went into battle without helmet or gas mask, and his headquarters were usually only a thousand yards behind the most forward trench. Wounded twice, he was decorated 13 times for bravery under fire during World War I. He became the 42nd's commanding officer and was promoted to brigadier general. By war's end, Secretary of War Newton D. Baker called MacArthur "America's best front-line general" of the war.

After the war ended, MacArthur returned to West Point as its new superintendent, the youngest ever to be given that post.

He modernized the academy's military training program before his tour of duty at the Point ended in 1922. For the next three years he held various commands in the Philippines, then returned to the United States in 1925. He was posted to the Philippines again between 1928 and 1930 and then served for the next five years as chief of the general staff.

In 1932, Dwight D. Eisenhower joined MacArthur's staff as a personal military assistant. "Ike" had mixed feelings about his superior officer, often disagreeing with MacArthur's policies. MacArthur had a reputation among his officers of being dictatorial. One of those in his command said, "If [Roman Emperor Julius] Caesar didn't look like MacArthur, he should have."

In 1935, President Franklin Delano Roosevelt appointed MacArthur as the military adviser to Philippine President Manuel Quezon to help develop an army for the U.S. possession, which had advanced to commonwealth status that year. MacArthur asked for and got Eisenhower as his assistant.

While MacArthur supervised organization of the Filipino Army, Eisenhower supervised building of a new airfield.

The two had different personalities; Ike made friends easily, while MacArthur was formal and appeared to be aloof. Often they disagreed on solutions to problems. By the time Ike was recalled to the United States in 1937, their relationship had become strained.

MacArthur retired from the army as a full general in 1937, at the age of 57, in order to accelerate the promotion of junior officers. That April he married Jean Marie Faircloth, a Tennessee heiress, and the following year she gave birth to a son, Arthur.

MacArthur took a new job as a field marshal in the Philippine Army. His close association with the Philippine people and leaders helped him to gain their respect, while at the same time he learned more of Japan's military buildup and territorial ambitions in the Pacific.

MacArthur considered the Philippines to be of utmost importance to the Japanese. At one of his staff conferences before leaving the army, he said the islands were the key that unlocked the door to the Pacific.

He knew that the Japanese understood this, for the Philippines, while not of great economic importance in Japan's master plan to control the western Pacific, was strategically of great importance. The islands were close to South China and the island stronghold of Formosa. The Philippines would provide the Japanese with a powerful strategic springboard for their drive southward and southeast. The islands were also highly important to the Allies, to protect and supply their own bases in Southeast Asia and the Southwest Pacific, as well as for striking back at the only potential enemy in the region— Japan. Whoever controlled the Philippines virtually controlled the area.

In July 1941, MacArthur was recalled to active duty as a major general in the U.S. Army, and was made commander-in-chief of the combined forces in the Philippines, which numbered about 35,000 American servicemen and 65,000 Filipinos.

He learned of the Japanese sneak attack on Pearl Harbor in Hawaii by means of a long-distance telephone call from Washington on December 8, the morning after the devastating raid. No details were given, but MacArthur knew Pearl Harbor was America's strongest military garrison in the Pacific, with its best aircraft deployed from strongly defended fields and with anti-aircraft batteries backed up by the U.S. Pacific Fleet. "My first impression was that the Japanese might well have suffered a serious setback," MacArthur wrote in his autobiography, *Duty, Honor, Country.*

At 9:30 A.M., reconnaissance planes reported enemy bombers heading toward Manila, the largest city and chief port in the Philippines. American pursuit planes were sent up to intercept them, but the Japanese bombers veered off without contact.

Soon MacArthur learned that the Japanese attack on Pearl Harbor had dealt the American base there a terrible blow. Then, at 11:45 A.M. a radio report alerted him that an overpowering formation of enemy planes was closing in on Clark Field, near Manila.

"Our fighters went up to meet them, but our bombers were slow in taking off and our losses were heavy," MacArthur wrote in his autobiography. "Our force was simply too small to smash the odds against them."

To take the Philippines, the Japanese deployed their Fourteenth Army from Formosa (today called Taiwan), numbering about 65,000 men and including two very strong divisions that had fought in China. The invading troops were supported by heavy air cover and the Japanese Third Fleet, which included five cruisers and four destroyers, plus a support task force standing by consisting of two aircraft carriers, five cruisers, and 13 destroyers.

MacArthur and Eisenhower had devised the basic strategic and tactical plans for the defense of the Philippines, intending total resistance to invaders, though they had fewer planes and ships at their command to support ground troops, and the Filipinos were not sufficiently trained to fight a major battle.

Japanese air strikes on December 8 destroyed most of the U.S. aircraft on the island of Luzon, largest and most important of the islands in the Philippines. The planes had been on the ground packed wing-to-wing as a protection against sabotage. Four days later, because of lack of air cover, U.S. Admiral Thomas Hart, commander of the Asiatic Fleet in Filipino waters, dispatched his ships to the Dutch East Indies for safety. They were later destroyed in the battle of the Java Sea.

The Japanese Fourteenth Army was put ashore on Luzon and began an advance directly south on Manila, capital of the Philippines. MacArthur's men valiantly tried to defend the city against the attackers, but the Japanese then began another large-scale landing.

As determined as MacArthur was, and as hard as the Americans and Filipinos fought, the defense of Manila was all but a lost cause. Through no fault of the defenders, the navy was unable to provide MacArthur with the supplies he needed. Without the necessary support, and against Japanese superiority in air power, tanks, and artillery, MacArthur was forced to retreat. Manila was evacuated on Christmas Eve, and Mac-

Arthur moved his headquarters to Corregidor, an island two miles square at the entrance to Manila Bay, just off the Bataan Peninsula.

MacArthur at this time became recognized as a somewhat theatrical soldier. He had already taken liberties with his military uniform in World War I, but now he had a new image in the war in the Pacific. He was often photographed wearing sunglasses and with a corncob pipe in his mouth. They became as familiar to fighting men in the Pacific and to civilians reading their newspapers back in the United States as was the eagle atop any American flagpole. Despite these affectations, MacArthur was considered a heroic leader in the defense of the Philippines.

The Bataan Peninsula, about 30 miles long and 15 wide, dominated by two high jungle-covered mountains, was short of supplies, but MacArthur hoped the troops gathered there could still defend the islands. However, overpowering Japanese forces soon forced the defenders to give up half their territory.

From Bataan, MacArthur fought for time, hoping to delay the Japanese advance southward until Australia could be adequately protected. General Eisenhower, meanwhile, did what little he could in Washington to facilitate the holding action by having more supplies sent to the islands.

Filipino morale began to sink as rumor spread that Washington had virtually given up on defending the Pacific until the war in Europe could be won. Fanning the flames of discouragement, "Tokyo Rose," a Japanese disc jockey, began broadcasting over the radio that those defending the Philippines were doomed to defeat and death while America's aid went to fight the Germans in Europe.

The Japanese began heavy bombing strikes over Corregidor. A 500-pound burst took the roof off MacArthur's headquarters. He moved it to a tunnel carved deep into a mountain. Then enemy air strikes and constant artillery bombardment took their toll in American and Filipino dead and injured.

MacArthur described the scene in his *Reminiscences:*

Our troops were now approaching exhaustion. The guerrilla movement was going well, but on Bataan and Corregidor the clouds were growing darker. My heart ached as I saw my men [Filipino soldiers] slowly wasting away. Their clothes hung on them like tattered rags. Their bare feet stuck out in silent protest. Their long bedraggled hair framed gaunt bloodless faces. Their hoarse, wild laughter greeted the constant stream of obscene and ribald jokes issuing from their parched, dry throats. They cursed the enemy and in the same breath cursed and reviled the United States; they spat when they jeered at the Navy.

But their eyes would light up and they would cheer when they saw my battered, and much reviled in America, "scrambled egg" cap. They would gather round and pat me on the back and "Mabuhay Macarsar" me. They would grin—that ghastly skeleton-like grin of the dying—as they would roar in unison, "We are battling bastards of Bataan—no papa, no mama, no Uncle Sam."

They asked no quarter and they gave none. They died hard—those savage men—not gently like a stricken dove folding its wings in peaceful passing, but like a wounded wolf at bay, with lips curled back in sneering menace, and always a nerveless hand reaching for that long sharp machete knife which long ago they had substituted for the bayonet. And round their necks, as we buried them, would be a thread of dirty string with its dangling crucifix. They were filthy, and they were lousy, and they stank. And I loved them.

MacArthur's wife and three-year-old son, Arthur, were with him in the Philippines, and both Philippine President Manuel Quezon and U.S. Army Chief of Staff General George C. Marshall suggested his loved ones be evacuated by submarine. Jean MacArthur refused to leave, and MacArthur told the others, "She will stay with me to the end. We drink from the same cup."

On February 20, President Quezon and his wife prepared to leave by submarine for safety in Australia. Before leaving, Quezon gave MacArthur the signet ring he always wore and said, "When they find your body, I want them to know you fought for my country."

The following day, General Marshall notified MacArthur that President Roosevelt was considering ordering MacArthur southward to Mindanao to set up a new base of operations for the defense of the southern part of the Philippines. On the same day, the government in Australia requested MacArthur's immediate assignment there as supreme commander of the newly formed Southwest Pacific Area. Roosevelt then sent MacArthur a personal message ordering him to proceed as soon as possible to Mindanao, do what he could to build up defenses there, and then go on to Australia.

"My first reaction was to try and avoid the latter part of the order," MacArthur wrote in his *Reminiscences*, "even to the extent of resigning my commission and joining the Bataan force as a simple volunteer. But my entire staff would have none of it."

MacArthur decided to try to reach Mindanao not by submarine but by breaking through a Japanese blockade with a fleet of PT boats. First he sent for General Jonathan M. Wainwright, who would be left in command. They had been at West Point together.

"He was a fine soldierly figure, he had already done wonders in the campaign, and was popular with both officers and men," MacArthur wrote. " 'Jim,' I told him, 'hold on till I come back for you.' I was to come back, but it would be too late—too late for those battling men in the foxholes of Bataan, too late for the valiant gunners at the batteries of Corregidor, too late for Jim Wainwright."

Under heavy enemy artillery fire, MacArthur, his wife, and his son left Corregidor early on the evening of March 11 and started for Mindanao in one of four small, battle-scarred PT boats.

A perilous journey followed, in choppy seas and within close range of the Japanese fleet. After three days the boats arrived safely at various beachheads on the east coast of Mindanao, the southernmost of the Philippine Islands. On March 16, before boarding a B-17 that would take him and his family to Australia, MacArthur made a statement for reporters:

"The President of the United States ordered me to break through the Japanese lines and proceed from Corregidor to Australia for the purpose, as I understand it, of organizing the

American offensive against Japan, a primary object of which is the relief of the Philippines. I came through and I shall return."

In *Reminiscences,* MacArthur wrote, "I spoke casually enough, but the phrase 'I shall return' seemed a promise of magic to the Filipinos. It lit a flame that became a symbol which focused the nation's indomitable will and at whose shrine it finally attained victory and, once again, found freedom. It was scraped in the sands of the beaches, it was daubed on the walls of the barrios, it was stamped on the mail, it was whispered in the cloisters of the church. It became the battle cry of a great underground swell that no Japanese bayonet could still."

General Wainwright remained behind to command in the Philippines, with Major General Edward King commanding the Bataan forces. Rations, which had been cut to half from the outset, now were cut again to a quarter, and by late March, about 25,000 men were sick.

In the meantime, reinforcements had reached the Japanese in the Philippines and another heavy attack began on April 3. After six days of hard fighting, King was forced to surrender his 76,000 men unconditionally.

The fall of Bataan left only the fortress island of Corregidor remaining for the Japanese to take, defended by General Wainwright and some 13,000 men. In the weeks that followed, Corregidor was subjected to one of the most intense continuous bombardments of the war. Its surface was churned to rubble and the garrison was forced into caves and tunnels. Reduced to three days' water and dwindling food supplies, and after 98 days of fighting against the greatest odds, Wainwright surrendered unconditonally on May 6, followed by other detachments over the course of about a week.

Wainwright, together with about 3,500 U.S. and Filipino troops, medical personnel, and civilians, was forced onto an infamous "Death March" to prison camps near Cabanatuan, a city about 60 miles north of Manila. Thousands died on the

march, while many more died during three years of imprison-
ment that followed.

Japanese forces in the taking of the Philippines had numbered about 50,000, against a U.S. 1st and 2nd Corps totaling
35,000 men, plus some 65,000 Filipinos. Twelve-thousand
Japanese had been killed in the fighting, and 16,000 Americans and Filipinos were killed or wounded, while 84,000 had
been taken as prisoners of war. The surrender of Bataan and
Corregidor was the largest capitulation in United States
military history, and completed the Japanese conquest of the
Philippines.

MacArthur arrived in Australia to find it desperately in need
of defense against the Japanese, since most young Aussies were
away, helping fight the Germans in Europe and North Africa.
Under MacArthur's leadership, American ships, men, and supplies began to arrive. Shortly after the fall of Corregidor, the
great battle of the Coral Sea was fought from May 4 to May 8,
1942. It was the Allies' first victory over Japan, and turned the
tide in the war. The battle of Midway followed a month later
when Admiral Chester Nimitz scored a victory over the Japanese on June 4.

In July, MacArthur's own troops began their first offensive
in the New Guinea campaign, pushing the Japanese out of
eastern New Guinea. He then directed the long campaigns with
the U.S. Seventh Fleet that led to the liberation of the Philippines. On October 16, 1944, aboard the *Nashville*, flagship of
what MacArthur called the most crucial naval battle of the war
in the Pacific, he witnessed one of the greatest armadas in
history, 282 ships of war carrying 174,000 American fighting
men. Under cover of night, the ships reached Leyte, above
Mindanao in the Philippines, and waited until dawn before
entering Leyte Gulf.

The guns of the American ships opened fire at dawn, the
Nashville knifed into the gulf, and the battle to reclaim the
Philippines began. The battle of Leyte Gulf was called the
greatest naval engagement of all time, and the American naval
forces destroyed the Japanese fleet. The engagement cost the

American fleet one light cruiser, two escort carriers, and three destroyers, but the armada sank four Japanese carriers, three battleships, six heavy cruisers, three light cruisers, and eight destroyers. MacArthur's 17 divisions defeated 23 Japanese divisions; GIs took 7,000 prisoners, and inflicted more than 300,000 casualties while suffering a loss of 60,628 Americans, including those wounded or missing. MacArthur had personally gone ashore with the first and second waves of landings.

After driving the Japanese off, MacArthur joined the G.I.s on the beach near Tacloban on the eastern shore of Leyte in the Philippines. With some enemy snipers still in the undergrowth not many yards away, he broadcast these words by radio:

People of the Philippines: I have returned. By the grace of Almighty God, our forces stand again on Philippine soil—soil consecrated in the blood of our two peoples. We have come, dedicated and committed to the task of destroying every vestige of enemy control over your daily lives, and of restoring upon a foundation of indestructible strength, the liberties of your people . . .

Rally to me. Let the indomitable spirit of Bataan and Corregidor lead us on. As the lines of battle roll forward to bring you within the zone of operations, rise and strike. Strike at every favorable opportunity. For your homes and hearths, strike! For future generations of your sons and daughters, strike! In the name of your sacred dead, strike! Let no heart be faint. Let every arm be steeled. The guidance of Divine God points the way. Follow in His name to the Holy Grail of righteous victory.

While the war in the Pacific continued, MacArthur was promoted to the new rank of general of the army (five-star general) in December 1944 and named to command all U.S. Army forces in the Pacific, comprising 22 divisions as well as six Marine divisions. On January 9, 1945, MacArthur led the liberation of Luzon and again waded ashore as he had at Leyte, this time to free the men of Bataan and Corregidor who were imprisoned there. It was to be his last battle of the war.

The following March, Corregidor was recaptured by U.S. paratroopers and shore landing parties. While the war in the Pacific continued and MacArthur and other military leaders made plans for new attacks that might speed the end of the conflict, on August 7, 1945, President Harry S Truman broadcast the following statement over the radio:

Sixteen hours ago an American airplane dropped one bomb on Hiroshima, an important Japanese army base. This bomb had more power than 20,000 tons of TNT. With this bomb we have now added a new and revolutionary increase in destruction to supplement the growing power of our armed forces. It is an atomic bomb. It is a harnessing of the basic power of the universe. We are now prepared to obliterate more rapidly and completely every productive enterprise the Japanese have above ground in any city. We shall destroy their docks, their factories, and their communications.

Let there be no mistake; we shall completely destroy Japan's power to make war. It was to spare the Japanese people from utter destruction that the ultimatum of July 26 was issued at Potsdam.

General Douglas MacArthur and aide Col. Lloyd Lehrabas view the results of a heavy naval bombardment that paved the way for the invasion of Los Negros Island in the Admiralties, February 29, 1944.
(U.S. Army Military History Institute)

On August 9, a second atomic bomb destroyed the city of Nagasaki, and the next day the Japanese announced they would surrender.

MacArthur accepted the surrender of Japan on the U.S.S. *Missouri* in Tokyo Harbor on September 25. Among those at the ceremony were General Wainwright, who had survived a prison camp in Manchuria.

MacArthur was then named supreme commander of the Allied powers in Japan and directed the Allied occupation of Japan. The general claimed to have no presidential ambitions, but was seriously considered for the Republican presidential nomination in 1948. His parents and grandparents had come from Wisconsin, and he considered that his home state. MacArthur's defeat in the Wisconsin state presidential primary discouraged his supporters, but four years later he rallied to help his former aide, Dwight Eisenhower, win their party's 1952 nomination and then the election.

Soon after the start of the Korean War in 1950, MacArthur was appointed commander of United Nations military forces in South Korea, while retaining his command of Allied forces in Japan. After driving the North Korean forces back over the 38th parallel, the prewar boundary between the two Koreas, he received President Truman's permission to press into North Korea and advance all the way to the Yalu River, the border between North Korea and communist China, despite warnings that this might provoke Chinese intervention.

China did intervene, causing the UN forces to fall back in disarray, and MacArthur asked permission to bomb Chinese bases in Manchuria. Truman refused permission. After MacArthur debated the issue publicly, the president removed him from command in April 1951.

The incident caused a public sensation and reminded many of how controversial a figure MacArthur was. His defenders said yes, he might be conceited and prone to press his judgment over even the president's, but he was still and always would be considered a master military strategist.

On his return to the United States, MacArthur received a hero's welcome. In concluding an address to a joint session of Congress, he spoke his famous words:

> *I am closing my fifty-two years of military service. When I joined the Army even before the turn of the century, it was the fulfillment of all my boyish hopes and dreams. The world has turned over many times since I took the oath on the Plain at West Point, and the hopes and dreams have long since vanished. But I still remember the refrain of one of the most popular barrack ballads of that day which proclaimed most proudly that—"Old soldiers never die, they just fade away." And like the old soldier of that ballad, I now close my military career and just fade away—an old soldier who tried to do his duty as God gave him the light to see that duty. Good-by.*

A triumphant tour of the United States followed, and MacArthur was cheered wherever he went, by some of the largest crowds ever gathered in those cities.

Another attempt to nominate MacArthur for president was unsuccessful in 1952, and he retired from active service to become an officer of Remington Rand, a large business corporation.

MacArthur and his wife led a quiet life though he remained active in politics. On May 12, 1962, he was awarded the Sylvanus Thayer Medal, the highest honor of the United States Military Academy. That day at West Point he told the graduating cadets,

"Duty—Honor—Country. Those three hallowed words reverently dictate what you ought to be, what you can be, what you will be."

MacArthur died April 5, 1964, in Walter Reed Army Hospital in Washington, D.C., from acute kidney and liver failure. The flag over the White House was lowered to half-mast and President Lyndon B. Johnson said, "One of the most distinguished soldiers in the history of the United States has died." After a state funeral and bestowal of the grateful nation's highest honors, MacArthur's body was taken to the courthouse at

Norfolk, Virginia, which has since been dedicated as a memorial to the general.

Douglas MacArthur was one of the most controversial military leaders in American history. Though a great soldier and leader of men in wartime, he was criticized for being vain, arrogant, and for sometimes challenging the orders of those over him in command.

He was, perhaps above all else, a paradox—and one of the most gifted generals in the history of the United States.

Chronology

January 26, 1880	born in Little Rock, Arkansas
1903	graduates from West Point; commissioned a second lieutenant
1906	appointed aide to President Theodore Roosevelt
1913	appointed to general staff
1917	promoted to colonel; assigned to Rainbow Division as chief of staff
1918	decorated for bravery fighting in France in World War I
1919	becomes superintendent of West Point
1930	becomes army chief of staff
1936	resigns from army; becomes Philippine field marshal
1937	marries Jean Marie Faircloth
1941	recalled to active duty as U.S. Far East commander; after Pearl Harbor attack, withdraws to Bataan and Corregidor
1942	leaves Philippines vowing to return; transferred to Australia, leading its defense against Japanese
1944	becomes a five-star general; commands successful invasion of Leyte in Philippines
1945	leads campaigns to regain Manila, Bataan, Corregidor; receives Japanese surrender on battleship

	Missouri; takes charge of occupation of Japan
1950	becomes commander of United Nations military force in South Korea
1951	removed from command in Korea by President Truman; returning home, he tells Congress "old soldiers never die, they just fade away"
1952	unsuccessful candidate for president; retires from active duty to become a businessman
1962	awarded Thayer Medal, West Point's highest honor
April 5, 1964	dies at Walter Reed Army Hospital, Washington, D.C.

Further Reading

Books by Douglas MacArthur
Duty, Honor, Country. New York: McGraw-Hill, 1965. Pictorial autobiography with 60,000 of the general's own words and over 200 photographs.

Reminiscences. New York: McGraw-Hill, 1964. A biography and history of his life and career in his own words.

Books About Douglas MacArthur
Darby, Jean. *Douglas MacArthur.* Minneapolis: Lerner, 1989. Good general biography for teenage readers.

Devaney, John. *Douglas MacArthur: Something of a Hero.* New York: Putnam, 1979. Concise narrative biography for teens.

Finkelstein, Norman. *The Emperor General.* Minneapolis: Dillon Press, 1989. Short, easy-to-read biography for teens.

Manchester, William. *American Caesar.* Boston: Little, Brown, 1978. Comprehensive, exciting one-volume biography.

Whitney, Maj. Gen. Courtney. *MacArthur—His Rendezvous with History.* New York: Alfred Knopf, 1956. Personal biography of MacArthur written by his staff officer in Australia during World War II and afterward in Japan.

Article About Douglas MacArthur
Current Biography, 1948. New York: H.W. Wilson, 1948. Biography of MacArthur up to 1948.

Admiral Chester W. Nimitz (1885–1966) Commander of U.S. Pacific Fleet

Admiral Chester W. Nimitz in 1945.
(Courtesy of FADM Nimitz; U.S. Naval Historical Center)

*A*dmiral Chester W. Nimitz began his service in World War II by getting one of the toughest assignments in American military history. He was ordered to replace Admiral Husband E.

Kimmel who had been relieved of command of the Pacific Fleet after the disastrous attack on Pearl Harbor, Hawaii, by the Japanese on December 7, 1941.

One of the navy's best-trained commanders, and also one of its best strategists and administrators, Nimitz took on the monumental task of rebuilding America's strength in the Pacific and, as the commander of the Pacific Fleet, led the United States naval forces to victory.

Chester W. Nimitz was born February 24, 1885, in Fredericksburg, Texas, a few months after his father had died. After a few years, the family moved to Kerrville, Texas, where he attended public schools and his mother married his late father's brother, William Nimitz.

Nimitz left high school after his third year, in 1901. He wanted to become a cadet at West Point, but appointments were all filled for the new class. He thought of Annapolis next, and won nomination to the Class of 1905.

At the Naval Academy, Nimitz, who was then a lean 150 pounds, excelled in both tennis and boxing, and became a stroke on the varsity crew team. But during his first year at Annapolis, he got seasick on a Sunday sailboat outing. Years later he confessed his "seagoing aspirations were very nearly obliterated."

Nimitz was popular with his fellow midshipmen, partly because he told Texas-sized tall tales and sometimes defied regulations at parties by drinking something stronger than punch. As a student, he had to study hard to make up for missing a final year of high school. Making matters worse, he came down with pneumonia in his first year at Annapolis and spent a month in the hospital, falling behind in classwork. Nevertheless, after four years of diligent study, he graduated seventh in a class of 114.

Nimitz's first assignment was aboard the U.S.S. *Ohio* at San Francisco. Promoted to ensign two years later, he asked to be assigned to a battleship, but instead was posted to a submarine, while subs were still in their infancy. He later commanded several submarines; in 1910, while captain of the *Skipjack*, a fireman who couldn't swim fell overboard and Nimitz rescued him, winning a Silver Life Saving Medal.

Nimitz studied at the diesel engine shops in Belgium and Germany, then spent over two years at the Navy Yard in New York City. In 1913 he married Catherine Vance Freeman of Wollaston, Massachusetts. He remained at the Navy Yard for several more years and built diesel engines for the oil tanker *Maumee* while stationed there. Promoted to the rank of lieutenant commander in 1916, he was made the *Maumee*'s executive officer and chief engineer.

The following August, about five months after the United States entered World War I, Nimitz was assigned to the staff of Admiral Samuel S. Robison, commander of the U.S. submarine force in the Atlantic Fleet. In his own words, Nimitz's war duties consisted "mainly of getting our submarines ready and then across the Altantic to operate with the Allies." While he did not see action in the war, Nimitz was given a citation for his fine work. He came to believe strongly in the value of submarines in modern warfare.

In the years before World War II, Nimitz served on both submarines and battleships, attended the Naval War College in Newport, Rhode Island, and became chief of the Bureau of Navigation at the Navy Department in Washington, D.C. He was in that position, in charge of setting up a new officer training program, when news came on December 7, 1941, that the Japanese had attacked Pearl Harbor on the Hawaiian island of Doha and devastated the United States base there. Nineteen ships including eight battleships were sunk or severely damaged, 188 U.S. aircraft were destroyed, 2,280 military personnel were killed and 1,109 wounded, and 68 civilians were also killed and many more wounded—a total of some 4,500 casualties.

The Bureau of Navigation immediately went on war alert. Nimitz began mobilizing the naval reserves. Ten days after the surprise attack on Pearl Harbor, Rear Admiral Nimitz was promoted to admiral and ordered to replace Admiral Husband E. Kimmel, who had been relieved of his command after the raid. Nimitz was given the crucial post on the recommendation of Admiral William D. Leahy, President Franklin D. Roosevelt's own chief of staff, who assured him Nimitz had never done a job that wasn't outstanding. "Tell Nimitz," said Roosevelt, "to get the hell out to Pearl and stay there till the war is won."

Nimitz was rushed to Hawaii by the fastest transport plane and didn't even have time to pack his admiral's uniform. Arriving in civilian clothes, the duty officer questioned who he was. Always cool and in command, Nimitz simply told him, "My name's Nimitz."

As commander-in-chief of the U.S. Pacific Fleet, Nimitz returned to the scene of earlier training and experience and immediately met with other admirals to plan war strategy. The plans were top secret and kept from the public, so in the first anxious days and weeks following the Japanese attacks on Pearl Harbor, Guam, and other U.S. bases, when reporters asked "What is the Pacific Fleet doing?" Nimitz answered *"Hoomana wa nui,"* an Hawaiian phrase meaning, "be patient."

Nimitz's first major victory against the Japanese fleet was at the battle of the Coral Sea in May 1942, in the southwest part of the Pacific Ocean between Australia, New Guinea, and the New Hebridies. The battle, fought mainly by aircraft near the Louisiade Archipelago, checked the southward expansion of the Japanese.

Nimitz then masterminded strategy for the great naval battle of Midway. Part of the victory in that decisive battle was due to his abilities in military deception.

As a student of naval strategy, Nimitz suspected the next Japanese target was to be Midway, a small coral atoll over a thousand miles northwest of Honolulu, and devised a scheme whereby he might become certain. Allied naval cryptographers had broken the Japanese naval radio code, and intercepted messages revealed that Japanese Admiral Isoroku Yamamoto planned to launch two thrusts, one a diversionary feint at Alaska, the other a major strike at an island in the Pacific identified only as "AF." That could mean any of the many strategic, Allied-held islands in the wide Pacific. But which one?

Nimitz ordered that an uncoded radio message be sent to Pearl Harbor reporting that Midway's water supply had broken down. The Japanese took Nimitz's bait. Three days later, Nimitz's radio operators intercepted a Japanese communication that mentioned that "AF's" water supply was not working.

Nimitz radioed Washington that he was certain the Japanese planned to attack Midway, but officials there said they believed the intercepted messages were part of a Japanese plan to trick U.S. strategists. Nimitz weighed the arguments at his Pearl Harbor headquarters, and decided Washington was wrong. The intercepted enemy messages, he believed, were authentic. He made his fleet plans accordingly. The result was the battle of Midway, June 4–6, 1942.

The day after the historic Allied victory at Midway, Nimitz's wireless operators handed him another deciphered Japanese message in which Yamamoto did not want to admit his defeat: OCCUPATION OF AF IS CANCELLED.

Nimitz laughed, telling his fellow officers, "Perhaps we will be forgiven if we claim we are about midway to our objective." After the pun, he said seriously, "Pearl Harbor has now been partially avenged."

The three-day air and sea battle of Midway was one of the decisive Allied victories of the war and a major turning point. It resulted in the destruction of four Japanese aircraft carriers, crippled the Japanese Navy, and sent Admiral Yamomoto to bed with a nervous breakdown. From Midway on, Japan was reduced to fighting a defensive war.

The victory at Midway was a huge morale booster for Americans everywhere, and Nimitz was called back to San Francisco to be awarded the Distinguished Service Medal by Admiral Ernest J. King, commander-in-chief of the U.S. Fleet.

Nimitz nearly lost his life when the seaplane flying him home crashed in San Francisco Bay. Nimitz was thrown into the chilly Golden Gate waters and the pilot died at the controls.

When a rescue launch picked up Nimitz, he exclaimed, "I'm all right, but for God's sake save my briefcase!" It was recovered, and he took its top secret contents with him to Admiral King.

King presented Nimitz with the Navy Distinguishing Service Medal, "Awarded for the successful actions against the enemy in the Coral Sea, May, 1942, and off Midway Island, June, 1942 . . . characterized by unfailing judgment and sound decision, completed with skill and vigor."

King and Nimitz were different types of commanders. Nimitz ran a tight but harmonious command, in contrast to the more bombastic "hell-and-thunder" of King's domain. Nimitz always avoided public displays of disharmony, keeping his negative thoughts about others to himself. He never got angry or upset in public and always welcomed differing opinions.

In 1942 Nimitz's command was expanded to include the entire Pacific Ocean. (A year later he was given the title fleet commander.) In August 1942, U.S. forces landed on Guadalcanal, a small but strategically important tropical island in the Solomon Islands northeast of Australia. At the same time, Lt. Col. Evans Carlson and his Marine "Raiders" waged guerrilla warfare against the enemy in the jungles of Makin Island in the Gilbert Group, to divert Japanese attention from the invasion of Guadalcanal.

After three months of fierce jungle fighting, Nimitz decorated 34 heroes of Guadalcanal, and commented that the U.S. forces had learned very quickly how to fight jungle warfare. In *Nimitz,* his biographer E.B. Potter said Nimitz was confident that "we can hold what we have got and consolidate our positions and eventually start moving ahead."

He concluded by saying, "I have always been optimistic regarding the eventual result of the war. Having seen the people on the spot, I have every reason to continue my optimism. This does not mean that we have the Japanese on the run, but it means that I have the utmost confidence that the men on the spot will hold what they have and eventually start rolling northward."

Marines on Guadalcanal were up against a fanatical, often suicidal enemy, and also suffered hunger, fatigue, and disease. Large Japanese naval forces converged on the island but were beaten off by Nimitz' navy with heavy losses to both sides. Eventually an entire Japanese troop convoy was sunk and the enemy began to weaken.

Guadalcanal was recaptured the following February by U.S. Marines after six hard months of fighting, and the Solomons proved to be as far south as the Japanese were able to advance.

In December 1942, on the anniversary of the attack on Pearl Harbor, Nimitz told reporters at a press conference that the United States forces would sweep the Japanese from the Aleutian islands, a chain of rugged volcanic islands off the Alaska Peninsula. He was still optimistic about the outcome of the war, but predicted a long struggle that would require more sacrifices on everyone's part.

During the time the Marines fought it out on Guadalcanal, General MacArthur lead an attack on the Japanese in New Guinea, an island a thousand miles long that was very important to the Japanese defense. What turned the tide for the Allies (Australians and Americans) was a series of heavy attacks from carrier-based aircraft, followed by heavy bombardment from the sea and finally, troop landings.

In the summer of 1944, Nimitz's fleet attacked the Marshall Islands and then the Marianas. The Japanese fleet was defeated and fled in a battle between carrier aircraft. The islands of Truk, Saipan, Guam, and Tinian were then captured by the Americans. As U.S. forces pushed northward, air bases were established and planes began bombing cities in Japan itself.

General Douglas MacArthur then began his campaign to reclaim the Philippines. Americans landed on Leyte Island in October and the battle of Leyte Gulf followed, one of the greatest naval engagements ever fought, in which U.S. naval forces under Admiral William "Bull" Halsey destroyed the Japanese fleet. The Philippine Islands were reconquered, and the United States regained mastery of the Pacific Ocean.

One of the last great battles of the war followed, in which U.S. Marines fought hard to capture Iwo Jima, an island about 700 miles from Tokyo. After shelling from ships offshore commanded by Admiral Raymond A. Spruance, and heavy bombardment by U.S. planes from aircraft carriers nearby, Marines landed on the beaches on February 19, 1945. Nearly two months of ground fighting would follow, but in March, Marines raised the Stars and Stripes on the summit of Mount Suribachi to symbolize their determination to capture Iwo Jima. There would be heavy American losses before the Marines accomplished their purpose and subdued the Japanese defenders.

After atomic bombs were dropped on Hiroshima and Nagasaki that August and the war in the Pacific ended, Admiral Nimitz was aboard his flagship, the U.S.S. *Missouri*, in Yokohama Bay on September 2, 1945, to sign the Japanese surrender documents. Not one to take all the glory, Nimitz attributed victory in the Pacific to the efforts of many others, units as well as individual officers and men, rather than himself. He singled out special praise for the repair teams and service squadrons, saying, "If it had not been for our mobile supply and repair base and floating dry docks, we would literally have been sunk."

Throughout the war in the Pacific, Nimitz maintained the position of chief strategist and got along with even the most difficult fellow leaders such as General Douglas MacArthur.

The naval historian Samuel Eliot Morison said Nimitz was an advocate of the principle: "Give every dog two bites." If a commander made a mistake, Nimitz was almost certain to give him a second chance. That attitude stemmed, in part, from the fact that, many years earlier, he himself had run his destroyer aground in Manila Bay and had been given an admonition and a second chance. After that, he was seldom unsympathetic to the shortcomings of junior officers.

Admiral Nimitz never received the public adulation that other great military leaders of World War II enjoyed. This was in part because he never sought the attention that came to

*Fleet Admiral Chester W. Nimitz, chief of naval operations, watches a
demonstration of anti-submarine weapons on board U.S.S.* Wiltsie *in the
Atlantic, May 11, 1946.*
(Courtesy of FADM Nimitz; U.S. Naval Historical Center)

General MacArthur because of his dramatics, or to his own
subordinate, Admiral Bull Halsey, because of his flamboyant
displays. Indeed, after the war, when just about every officer
of every service branch was writing an autobiography, Nimitz
declined offers from publishers. He said that work should be
left to historians, and it was only 10 years after his death that
his widow allowed a book to be published about his war years.

In December 1945 Nimitz succeeded Fleet Admiral King as chief of naval operations. Two years later he returned to California for special duties under the secretary of the navy.

In 1949 he was named to a United Nations post as administrator of Kashmir. President Harry S Truman brought him back to Washington in 1951, appointing him head of the provisional Internal Security Commission.

Nimitz believed his new job was as important as defending his country in wartime, saying, "The United States is no abstract authority residing in Washington. The United States is the average person who, like yourself, is living as an individual proud of his liberties, conscious of his responsibility to his neighbor, participating in his government, self-disciplined by education, and by education inspired to further God's will on earth."

Besides receiving his own country's highest honors, Nimitz was presented awards from 15 foreign nations and given honorary degrees from 19 American colleges and universities. He retired from the navy in 1948 and became regent of the University of California. He and his wife lived in Berkeley where he engaged in a favorite new hobby, gardening, which was perhaps ironic for someone whose life's work had been as a sailor.

The Nimitzes' son, Chester W. Nimitz Jr., also became a rear admiral, and of three daughters, one married a naval officer, Captain James T. Lay. Nimitz and his wife had been living on Yerba Buena Island in San Francisco Bay when he suffered a stroke and died on February 20, 1966, four days before his 81st birthday. He was buried where he asked to be, in Golden Gate National Cemetery alongside thousands of the sailors and soldiers who had served with him in the Pacific.

In *Nimitz,* E.B. Potter wrote:

The blue-eyed gentle Nimitz [was] hard as nails underneath, the professional naval officer who knew best of all how to get optimum performance from his major weapon: men.

Nimitz shared with that great soldier Dwight D. Eisenhower a disarming and almost misleading appearance of ordinariness and diffidence. Like Eisenhower, Nimitz was a master at delegation of authority. Nimitz had a quality unique to himself, too; there was always a sense of urgency and special responsibility to his delegations of authority. He wanted action, immediate, appropriate, and resultful action—and he nearly always got it.

Nimitz's great strength was his ability to coax the very best from others. One could say that Halsey was the man to win a battle for you, Spruance was the man to win a campaign, but Nimitz was the man to win a war.

Chronology

February 24, 1885	born in Fredericksburg, Texas
1901	appointed to U.S. Naval Academy
1905	graduates and serves aboard U.S.S. *Ohio* at San Francisco
1907	promoted to ensign; begins duty aboard submarines
1913	marries Catherine Vance Freeman; serves at Navy Yard in New York City
1916	promoted to lieutenant commander; becomes executive officer of the tanker *Maumee*
1917–18	aide to commander of submarine force in Atlantic Fleet
1919	commander of Submarine Division 14 at Pearl Harbor, Hawaii
1935–38	assistant chief of Bureau of Navigation
1938	promoted to rear admiral and commander of Cruiser Division 2, then Battleship Division One
1939	chief of Bureau of Navigation
1941	promoted to admiral and commander-in-chief of U.S. Pacific Fleet
1942	chief strategist for victorious battles of Coral Sea and Midway
1943	chief strategist for liberation of Guadalcanal and victory in Solomon Islands

1945	one of signers of Japanese surrender; becomes chief of Naval Operations
1947	assigned special duties under secretary of navy
1948	regent of University of California at Berkeley
1949	United Nations administrator of Kashmir
1951	head of Internal Security Commission
February 20, 1966	dies in San Francisco at age 80

Further Reading

Books About Chester W. Nimitz

Hoyt, Edwin P. *How They Won the War in the Pacific.* New York: Weybright and Talley, 1970. Comprehensive study of how Nimitz and others won the war in the Pacific.

Potter, E.B. *Nimitz.* Annapolis: Naval Institute Press, 1976. Authorized biography of Nimitz.

Article About Chester W. Nimitz

Current Biography, 1942. New York: H.W. Wilson, 1942. Summary of his life up to 1942.

Admiral William F. "Bull" Halsey (1882–1959) Commander, Third Fleet

Vice Admiral William F. Halsey Jr. as commander, Aircraft, Battle Force, 1941.
(U.S. Naval Historical Center)

*I*n November 1941, a month before the Japanese attack on Pearl Harbor, Hawaii, Vice Admiral William F. "Bull" Halsey was commander of the U.S. Pacific Fleet. More planes were needed to bolster the defense of Wake and Midway Islands to the west of Hawaii, since a Japanese attack somewhere in the Pacific was considered possible. Halsey was to take the planes there by aircraft carrier. The mission was to be kept top secret so the Japanese would not learn of the United States' defensive buildup.

Halsey was aboard the carrier *Enterprise,* returning from his mission and approaching Pearl Harbor at dawn on December 7, when the Japanese attacked the base. He had expected a battle, but not right under his nose at his home base. In the months and years ahead, he would play a leading role in the American naval battles that would determine the outcome of World War II in the Pacific.

William Frederick Halsey Jr. was born on October 30, 1882, in Elizabeth, New Jersey. There had been navy men in the family since 1704. Several had been captains of whaling ships. His father was a navy captain, and young Bill attended school at a variety of naval stations. When Bill was nine, his father became an instructor of physics and chemistry at the U.S. Naval Academy at Annapolis, Maryland. Young Bill loved life there and decided to become a navy officer when he grew up.

In 1900, Halsey became a cadet at Annapolis, where he became so popular, the class yearbook called him "everybody's friend." He excelled in athletics, especially football, but was a below-average student, ranking 43rd in a class of 62.

After graduating in 1904, Halsey served aboard a battle-ship, the U.S.S. *Missouri.* That spring, while the ship was in waters off Cuba, Halsey was on the bridge, watching practice firing, when a terrible accident occurred. Some bags containing gunpowder in the ammunition room below deck caught fire and exploded. Twenty-six enlisted men and five officers, including some of Halsey's closest friends, were killed. The disaster, which happened on May 13, left Halsey with night-marish memories and a strong dislike for the 13th of any month.

While the *Missouri* was undergoing repairs, Halsey was detached to the Naval Academy for temporary duty as assistant backfield football coach. Afterward, he served briefly back aboard the *Missouri* in 1905, then was transferred to a cruiser, the U.S.S. *Don Juan de Austria,* based at Norfolk, Virginia.

While drilling men on deck one afternoon in 1906, Halsey felt something soft hit him in the back of the head. His cap was knocked off, and his men began laughing. Looking around, Halsey saw a lady's muff lying on the deck. He discovered it had been thrown at him mischievously by a pretty young lady who had come aboard as a guest for tea with the executive officer's wife. When Halsey asked why she had thrown the muff at him, the young woman said it was because he seemed to take himself so seriously.

The woman was Frances Cooke Grandy, from Norfolk. Like Halsey, she came from a navy family. Halsey soon learned that her cousin, Wiley Grandy, was one of his best friends, and the couple began dating.

A second eventful thing happened for Halsey aboard the *Don Juan* in 1906. Two years and a day after his graduation from the Naval Academy, he was commissioned an ensign.

Halsey then served aboard the battleship *Kansas* in the Caribbean and in Atlantic Ocean waters off South America. With 15 other battleships, they were part of President Theodore Roosevelt's plan to show America's naval power in the area, an attempt to counteract Japan's growing interests there. Later, Halsey sailed with the ships to Japan at that country's invitation, then on to China before returning to the United States in 1909. Back home again, he and Miss Grandy were married later that year.

In the years that followed and up to World War I, Halsey served aboard a torpedo boat, a destroyer, and several other ships in the Caribbean. He was commander of the *Jarvis,* a destroyer stationed off Sandy Hook, New Jersey, when World War I broke out in August 1914.

Halsey's service during World War I was as captain of two different ships patrolling the North Sea approaches to England, which were menaced by German U-boats. After the war he attended both the Naval War College in Newport, Rhode Island, and the Army War College in Carlisle Barracks, Pennsylvania. Convinced of the importance of air power, Halsey learned to fly a plane at the Naval Air Station in Pensacola, Florida. He received his wings in 1935, then became captain of an aircraft carrier, the *Saratoga*.

Three years later, promoted to rear admiral, Halsey led an aircraft carrier task force—a group of battleships, destroyers, and other ships escorting and protecting carriers. In 1940, promoted to vice admiral, he took command of Aircraft, Battle Force in the Pacific, as well as the carrier division, and was in that duty when Pearl Harbor was attacked.

Halsey was six feet tall and weighed 160 pounds, with a heavy jaw, blue eyes, and thick eyebrows. Though he seemed gruff, by nature he was courteous, warm, and even sentimental. He was also superstitious; he feared Friday the 13th, carried many good luck charms, and knocked on wood for good luck.

Over 2,000 American military and civilian personnel had been killed in the sneak attack on Pearl Harbor, about half again that number were injured, and 19 U.S. ships were sunk or severely damaged. Only a dozen army patrol planes on Oahu had survived the attack. Admiral Husband E. Kimmel, commander in chief of the U.S. Pacific Fleet, ordered Halsey to strike back, but he had only one carrier, no battleships, and just a few planes, against the Japanese force of six carriers, countless battleships, and about 150 planes.

Washington officials blamed Kimmel for being unprepared for the surprise attack on Pearl Harbor. On December 17, he was relieved of his command and replaced by Rear Admiral Chester W. Nimitz, chief of the Bureau of Navigation.

The Japanese struck almost simultaneously at Guam, Wake Island, the Philippines, Hong Kong, and British Malaya, then followed the air raids with land invasions. Taking the Philippines was of vital interest to the Japanese. If the islands were under their control, this would not only prevent U.S. bombers and ships from using them as bases for attack, but would also allow the Japanese to use the islands as air and naval springboards to strike at Australia.

While MacArthur commanded the American resistance in the Philippines, Admiral Halsey was impatient to strike back at the Japanese, despite being greatly outnumbered in manpower and ships. Early in February 1942 he took the *Enterprise* and another carrier, *Yorktown*, plus four heavy cruisers, a light cruiser, and 10 destroyers to make a surprise raid of his own, on Japanese-held islands in the Marshall and Gilbert groups in the central Pacific, about halfway between the Philippines and the Hawaiian Islands.

The raids Halsey led were so successful that he was awarded the Navy Distinguished Service Medal. Newsmen began writing that he was the nemesis of the Japanese and nicknamed him "Bull" Halsey, implying he was ferocious as a bulldog. The navy had sunk 16 Japanese ships in the raids and newspaper headlines proclaimed, "Pearl Harbor Avenged!"

As the Japanese continued their efforts to take the Philippines, they also were poised to strike the Australian base of Port Moresby on the south coast of New Guinea. To divert the enemy, Halsey took Task Force 16 to bombard Wake Island, west of Hawaii, which the Japanese had taken after an heroic U.S. Marine defense the previous December. His ships consisted of three aircraft carriers, seven destroyers, and an oiler. Their air attacks caught the Japanese on Wake Island by surprise and caused heavy damage.

Halsey followed that action soon after with a highly successful strike at the Marcus Islands, northwest of Wake. After a brief illness, which sent him back stateside, he returned to the Pacific to resume command of aircraft carriers.

Meanwhile, months of Japanese air strikes and troop landings had overpowered the U.S. and Filipino defenders in the Philippines, and they were forced to surrender on April 9. American military leaders decided a blow had to be struck against the enemy that would speak for freedom and those who had suffered or lost their lives at Pearl Harbor, Bataan, and elsewhere in the Pacific. On April 18, 1942, Admiral Halsey led a task force that included the aircraft carrier *Hornet* from which James H. "Jimmy" Doolittle took off with 16 B-25 bombers to lead the first aerial raid on Tokyo. Japanese leaders had told their people that the homeland never would be bombed or invaded. Doolittle's daring raid proved them wrong.

After the fall of Corregidor to the Japanese on May 6, Admiral Nimitz made plans to counter an invasion of Midway, a strategically important island far northwest of the Hawaiian Islands. Halsey was eager to take part but was hospitalized with a case of dermatitis, a painful skin inflammation. He was forced to miss the battle of Midway on June 6, where the Japanese Navy suffered a crushing defeat from which it never fully recovered. Halsey became a full admiral in October 1942 and was named commander of the South Pacific area.

The Japanese Admiral Isoroku Yamamoto then sent his combined fleet against American naval forces operating in the Solomon Islands, between the Gilbert Islands and New Guinea. The Japanese force consisted of four battleships, three aircraft carriers, eight heavy cruisers, two light cruisers, and 29 destroyers. American naval forces were considerably smaller, only one battleship, two aircraft carriers, three heavy and three light cruisers, and 14 destroyers.

An American carrier task force headed for the Santa Cruz Islands, a small island group lying east of the Solomons, to be in position to intercept Japanese ships approaching Guadalcanal. In the air, gunnery, and torpedo battle that ensued as the Japanese and United States fleets fought each other in late October, three Japanese bombs struck Halsey's *Enterprise* but did only minor damage. The U.S. aircraft carrier *Hornet* was hit hard by torpedoes and was sunk.

The battle of Santa Cruz was important because Japanese losses prevented them from providing effective air support of their troops on Guadalanal. On February 6, 1943, Halsey led his task force in helping the Marines retake Guadalcanal, the largest offensive yet undertaken by the U.S. in the Pacific.

Admiral William F. "Bull" Halsey

In his biography, Halsey wrote that President Roosevelt, Admirals Nimitz and King and others sent him messages of congratulations, but he said he didn't deserve their praise. "I had no illusions about who deserved them," he said in *Admiral Halsey's Story,* "so I passed them on to the men who had done the fighting."

He did, however, appreciate Admiral Nimitz's appraisal of him, which appeared in the November 30, 1942, issue of *Time* magazine and bore the title "Battle of the Pacific: Hit Hard, Hit Fast, Hit Often," which was Halsey's famous motto. Nimitz wrote that:

> *Halsey's conduct of his present command leaves nothing to be desired. He is professionally competent and militarily aggressive without being reckless or foolhardy. He has that rare combination of intellectual capacity and military audacity, and can calculate to a cat's whisker the risk involved in operations when successful accomplishments will bring great returns. He possesses superb leadership qualities which have earned him a tremendous following of his men. His only enemies are Japs.*

After that, it seemed that Halsey and his men always accomplished the impossible. Far outnumbered by the Japanese, he called his own men and ships his "shoestring affair," often avoiding open combat but using speed and surprise to deal heavy blows against the enemy.

"We get away with it because we violate all the traditional rules of naval warfare," he explained in his autobiography. "We do the exact opposite of what they expect us to do. Most important, whatever we do, we do fast."

In June 1944, Halsey took command of the Third Fleet, which was called the most powerful naval striking force the world had ever known.

Halsey recommended the landing on Leyte Gulf in the Philippines that October, which President Roosevelt said caused a "complete change in the campaign plans for the Philippines." Almost the entire Japanese Navy took part in the battle, and suffered greater losses than in any other naval engagement in history. Historians have called the battle of Leyte Gulf one of the greatest naval engagements of all time, as American naval forces all but destroyed the Japanese fleet.

The battle took place between October 2 and December 31, 1944, at Leyte Gulf, which lies between Mindanao, Leyte, and Samar Islands in the Philippine Archipelago. The sea battles raged over a vast area of ocean around the Philippines, while land fighting was concentrated around the American bridgehead on Leyte. U.S. forces engaged were Admiral Halsey's Third Fleet and Admiral Thomas C. Kinkaid's Seventh Fleet, totaling about 148,000 seamen, and General Walter Krueger's U.S. Sixth Army of about 150,000 troops, against the Japanese combined fleet of 42,800 seamen and about 350,000 troops.

The battle took place because the Americans were closing in on Japanese-held territories in the Pacific. Island after small island was taken after hard-fought battles by the U.S. Marine Corps. By October 1944, Saipan, Guam, and other important islands had been either captured or retaken by the Marines, and American superiority in the air was growing. U.S. naval strength in the Pacific had grown to some 112 ships, including seven fleet and eight light carriers and seven battleships, to Japan's 55 ships, including five fleet and four light carriers, and five battleships. American naval aircraft totaled 956 to Japan's 573. To the Japanese military leaders, the handwriting was on the wall, and a major effort to stop the Americans was necessary.

In September, after raids on the Philippines by Admiral Halsey's fleet, President Roosevelt and Great Britain's Prime Minister Winston Churchill agreed to an invasion to liberate Manila and Luzon in the Philippines. As a preliminary to this, four U.S. carrier groups attacked Formosa (today called Taiwan), an island off the China coast, destroying 500 more Japanese aircraft at a cost of 76 American planes lost.

For the reconquest of the central Philippines, the United States assembled almost 740 ships including 17 aircraft carriers. Landings on Leyte, which began on October 20, were met with only light enemy opposition, and within two days,

Admiral William F. "Bull" Halsey

Adm. William F. Halsey Jr., commander of the Third Fleet, is shown deep in meditation on the bridge of U.S.S. New Jersey *while en route to the Philippines, December 1944.*
(National Archives)

132,000 U.S. troops and over 200,000 tons of supplies were safely ashore.

Two Japanese fleets then sailed out of the Inland Sea to meet the challenge. Heavy air and sea strikes followed on both sides as Admiral Halsey sought to engage in battle against Vice Admiral Jisaburo Ozawa's carriers sailing from Japan.

Early on October 25, Halsey's *Enterprise* was 300 miles north of Leyte while a fierce land-sea battle was taking place off Samar and closer to Leyte, as Vice Admiral Takeo Kurita's fleet challenged U.S. Admiral Clifton Sprague's escort carriers and destroyers. After suffering some losses, Sprague called up a massive air strike and Kurita withdrew.

Later that day, Halsey found action at last against Ozawa in the battle of Cape Engano, and by nightfall, all four Japanese carriers were sunk. But Halsey failed to block Kurita's escape route via the San Bernardino Channel, and a great opportunity to cause the Japanese even heavier losses was missed. It was apparent, however, that the Japanese plan for a major naval success had failed badly. The loss of the last four Japanese fleet carriers signaled the end of the naval war—won most decisively by the Americans.

U.S. casualties were 25,584 troops and 3,800 seamen, while Japanese casualties totaled 74,000 troops and 10,500 seamen. The American victory resulted eventually in winning the war in the Pacific and immediately in the virtual destruction of the Japanese fleet, as well as affording an important advance on land toward recapture of the Philippines.

Though Halsey was a hero of the Leyte Gulf battle, he also was criticized for endangering the Philippine invasion by engaging a small Japanese carrier force with few planes, thereby leaving the San Bernardino Straits unprotected. Halsey denied it was a tactical error, claiming that he could have inflicted even more damage on the Japanese fleet if he hadn't been pressured to turn back.

Halsey's record spoke for itself. From August 1944 to January 1945, his Third Fleet destroyed 4,370 enemy planes, sank 82 combat ships and 372 others, while losing 449 planes and a light cruiser.

Early in 1945, Halsey raided the China Sea, and his Third Fleet struck at the Japanese southern supply line for 11 days. In just one day, his ships sank 44 combat vessels and tankers as well as 112 enemy planes; 23 of his own aircraft were lost.

On January 27, 1945, Halsey had to leave the battle zone for a flight back to Pearl Harbor to attend a strategy briefing. In his autobiography, Halsey says General Douglas MacArthur wired him: "Your departure from this theater leaves a gap that can be filled only by your return."

Admiral William F. "Bull" Halsey

During a trip back to the United States in March, Halsey was awarded the Gold Star by President Roosevelt rather than a third Distinguished Service Medal. The citation with the award read: "Under his forceful and inspiring leadership, the recovery of the Philippines was painstakingly prepared for, covered and effectively supported during operations which evidenced his daring tactics and the devotion to duty of his gallant command."

In the closing weeks of the war, Halsey's command destroyed or damaged 2,804 Japanese planes, sank or damaged 148 combat ships and 1,598 supply ships, and struck hard blows on Japanese railroads and industry. In his autobiography, Halsey says these victories led Fleet Admiral King to say, "It helps explain the sudden collapse of Japan's will to resist."

Japan surrendered on September 2, 1945, aboard Halsey's flagship, the U.S.S. *Missouri.*

During many battles, Halsey told his men he hoped some day he would be able to ride Emperor Hirohito's white horse in Tokyo. After the war ended, American soldiers in Tokyo gave him a white army horse to ride when he reviewed the First Cavalry Division.

"Bull" Halsey had a reputation for being an aggressive fighter and leader, but also had great admiration and affection for his men. In his autobiography, he recalls his farewell message to the Third Fleet:

"I am so proud of you that no words can express my feelings. At times you were driven almost beyond endurance but only because the stakes were high, the enemy was weary as you were, and the lives of many Americans could be spared in later offensives if we did our work well now. Superlatively well done."

Halsey returned home a hero and was promoted to fleet admiral, a five-star admiral, in December 1945. He retired from the navy two years later, partly because of ill health, but also to give younger officers a chance to move up the promotion ladder.

He collaborated with Joseph Bryan in writing his autobiography, *Admiral Halsey's Story,* and entered private business, becoming chairman of the board of the American Cable and Radio Corporation. He died of a heart attack on August 6, 1959, while vacationing at Fisher's Island, New York.

Chronology

October 30, 1882	born in Elizabeth, New Jersey
1904	graduates from Annapolis
1906	commissioned an ensign in U.S. Navy
1909	marries Frances Cook Grandy
1914–18	captains patrol ships in North Sea
1935	receives wings; captains aircraft carrier *Saratoga*
1938	promoted to rear admiral
1940	promoted to vice admiral; takes command of Aircraft, Battle Force in Pacific
December 7, 1941	aboard carrier *Enterprise* approaching Pearl Harbor at time of Japanese air attack
1942	leads naval raids on Marshall and Gilbert islands, Marcus Island; heads task force from which Jimmy Doolittle bombs Tokyo; becomes full admiral; wins battle of Santa Cruz
1943	leads task force in retaking Guadalcanal
1944	commands Third Fleet in Pacific and leads battle of Leyte Gulf
1945	raids China Sea and strikes at Japan; receives Gold Star from President Roosevelt; witnesses Japanese surrender aboard U.S.S.

Missouri; promoted to five-star admiral

1947   retires, becomes businessman, and writes autobiography

August 6, 1959   dies of heart attack at Fisher's Island, New York

Further Reading

Book by William F. Halsey

Admiral Halsey's Story. New York: McGraw-Hill, 1947. Autobiography written with Joseph Bryan. Halsey's own account of his sometimes controversial career.

Books About William F. Halsey

Merrill, James M. *A Sailor's Admiral.* New York: Crowell, 1976. Not the most complete, but the easiest-to-read biography of Halsey by a navy historian.

———. *Target Tokyo.* Chicago, Rand McNally, 1964. Easy-to-read, detailed account of the Halsey-Doolittle raid on Tokyo.

General Dwight D. Eisenhower (1890–1969) Supreme U. S. Commander in Europe

General of the Army Dwight D. Eisenhower, supreme commander of the U. S. forces in the European Theater, 1945.
(U. S. Army Military History Institute)

*I*t was sunrise—6:30 on the morning of June 6, 1944. The world had been at war for almost five years, and Adolph Hitler's Nazi Germany still had a stranglehold on Europe.

General Dwight D. Eisenhower

From Allied command headquarters in London, England, a radio broadcast announced to the world: "Under the command of General Eisenhower, Allied naval forces supported by strong air forces began landing Allied armies this morning on the northern coast of France."

The first 150,000 American, British, Canadian and other Allied soldiers out of an invasion force that would swell to more than 1,361,000 had left the east coast of England to cross the English Channel and attempt a beachhead on the Nazi-occupied northwestern coast of France. Some 7,774 planes and 4,308 battleships, cruisers, destroyers and other ships would take part in the invasion. "Operation Overlord" was the largest planned military operation in history, and upon its success or failure lay the future of the free world.

The supreme commander of the Normandy invasion held perhaps the most important job in the largest war the world had ever known. Who was the man chosen for that job, upon which hung the fate of the free world? In many ways, Dwight David Eisenhower was an unlikely choice.

Eisenhower was born in Denison, Texas, on October 14, 1890. He grew up in Abilene, Kansas, where his father worked in a dairy, and got his nickname of "Ike" while in elementary school. After high school he worked and saved his money, but fearing that he wouldn't have the funds to pay for four years of college, Ike enrolled in the U.S. Military Academy at West Point.

Eisenhower felt like a poor farm boy among more sophisticated boys from around the country, but soon he became popular. His classmates liked his sense of humor, which he demonstrated by having some fun with the academy's rules. On one occasion, ordered to report to his quarters in "full dress coats," which meant complete formal uniform, he showed up in just his uniform coat and nothing underneath.

After graduation from West Point in 1915, Ike was commissioned a second lieutenant in the U.S. Army and assigned to the 19th Infantry Regiment at Fort Sam Houston, Texas. There he met Mamie Geneva Doud and they dated, but after several months, he was assigned to duty along the Mexican border as part of the U.S. Army's "punitive expedition" to capture the bandit chief, Pancho Villa. On one raid, guerrillas ambushed Ike and fired several shots his way, but they all missed. After that, his comrades gave him a new nickname, "Lucky Ike."

Upon his return, Eisenhower resumed his courtship of Mamie Doud. At the same time, he decided he wanted to learn to fly and become a pilot in the army's new air branch. But Mamie's father said this was a risky and irresponsible career move for a future son-in-law. Ike saw he had a choice to make. He decided Mamie meant more to him than flying, so he chose to stay in the infantry. He and Mamie were married on July 1, 1916, the same day he was promoted to first lieutenant.

The following April, the United States declared war on Germany and entered World War I.

Ike wanted to be sent overseas to fight, but because he had shown a strong ability to train men, he was assigned instead to train new recruits at Fort Oglethorpe, Georgia. Mamie gave birth to their son, Doud Dwight, while her husband was on training duty at a mock battlefield that fall. The next year, Eisenhower was transferred to Fort Meade in Maryland where he served with the 65th Engineers Tank Battalion.

Just before his 28th birthday, Ike finally got his wish to go overseas and fight. Mamie and their son returned to her hometown of Denver, Colorado, and Eisenhower was about to leave for Europe when the war ended. Germany signed the Armistice ending World War I on November 11, 1918, and Eisenhower's orders were cancelled. He complained to a junior officer, "I suppose we'll spend the rest of our lives explaining why we didn't get into this war."

Like many other army officers, Eisenhower's rank was cut after the war, from lieutenant colonel to captain, and he was put in charge of discharging thousands of men from the army. Discouraged, he thought of resigning his commission.

Reunited with his wife and son at Fort Meade, Ike's spirits lifted. He became good friends with another young officer at the camp. George Patton was feisty, a few years older, and had fought in the tank corps in France. Ike found that they shared a mutual enthusiasm for the future of tank warfare.

Through his friendship with Patton, Ike met General Fox Conner. During the war in Europe, Conner had been the right-hand man of General John J. Pershing, commander of the American Expeditionary Force. Conner became interested in the two younger officers' ideas about tank warfare.

Life was looking promising for Eisenhower when his son fell ill and died of scarlet fever. In his memoirs, *At Ease: Stories I Tell to Friends,* Ike wrote that the death of his son was the greatest disappointment and disaster of his life.

A few years later, in 1922, General Conner selected Eisenhower to be his executive officer, or second in command, in the Panama Canal Zone. Ike welcomed the overseas duty, especially since he could take his wife along.

Conner renewed Ike's interest in history, and he began reading more about military campaigns, battle strategy, and war philosophy. Years later, he said that what he learned from General Conner was equal to a graduate course in military affairs. This study gave him the foundation of knowledge that helped him to become one of the greatest military leaders in army history.

The Eisenhowers returned to Denver for the birth of their second son, John Sheldon, on August 3, 1922, then spent another three years in Panama. Ike then attended the Army War College in Carlisle Barracks, Pennsylvania, and learned more about military strategy. He served as assistant executive in the office of the secretary of war from 1929 to 1933. He then joined General Douglas MacArthur in the Philippines, from 1935 to 1940, helping organize a Philippine army.

During those years, Ike read much about the growing war fever in Europe. In 1939, after Great Britain and France declared war on Nazi Germany, he asked MacArthur to let him go back home, because he expected the United States soon to be drawn into the war. But MacArthur said he needed him in the Philippines. MacArthur's resistance was a bitter disappointment to Ike, who felt he had been cheated out of World War I. Now another world conflict had begun, and he worried he might not get to fight in it. It wasn't that he loved war; rather, he hated oppression and wanted to fight to restore and preserve freedom.

While supervising construction of a new airfield in the Philippines, Ike had a premonition that he would play an important role in the army if the United States should enter the war. A peacetime draft of young men into the armed services was approved by Congress, and to his great pleasure, in December 1939, Ike was reassigned to Fort Lewis, Washington, to instruct new recruits. Meanwhile, his son John had grown up and was a cadet at West Point.

After two years of training troops, Ike was promoted to colonel in September 1941 and sent to Louisiana where one of the most unexpected and important turning points in his life occurred. He took part in the army's "war games," in which two armies totaling 400,000 troops were to "fight" each other.

Ike was assigned to the chief of staff of the Third Army, to plan strategy for the maneuvers. Though the Second Army had more armored striking force, the Third Army won the battle. Ike received most of the credit.

Ike went back to Texas for a brief rest after the maneuvers. He went to bed and left orders not to be disturbed, but was awakened the next morning, December 7, 1941, only to learn that the Japanese had attacked Pearl Harbor. The next day, the United States declared war on Japan. On December 11, Japan's ally, Germany, declared war on the United States.

Ike's performance as a military strategist in the Louisiana "war games" won him promotion to brigadier general. General George C. Marshall, the army chief of staff, needed someone to plan war strategy. In 1942, he appointed Eisenhower as head of the newly created Operation Division of the War Department.

General Dwight D. Eisenhower

Ike was flattered, but he couldn't help but regret that he would be stuck behind a desk in the war and not get to see action himself. It didn't take him long, however, to realize the full extent of the challenge of his new job. He was to plan the army's strategy for winning the war in Europe.

As the war progressed and Germany's control of Europe and Africa tightened, Ike realized that a bold plan had to be devised. He began to formulate a plan that called for the Allies to invade France by crossing the English Channel. General Marshall agreed with it; so did President Franklin D. Roosevelt. With British approval, Marshall appointed Ike commander in charge of all American troops in Europe and gave him authority to finalize his invasion plan.

But when Ike arrived in London he learned that British Prime Minister Winston Churchill was opposed to an Allied invasion in 1942. He wanted Ike's invasion plan to wait until the Allies could regain control of the Mediterranean Sea from Germany and Italy, and oust the Germans from North Africa.

Ike had to put his European invasion plan on hold, but was given command of the entire Allied invasion of North Africa. He commanded the landings there in November 1942, with the American troops led by his old friend, George Patton, now also a general.

Afterward Ike successfully directed the invasions of Sicily the following July, and Italy in September. Seeing the destruction and lives lost in Europe, Ike's hatred for the Nazis intensified. He would later write in *Crusade in Europe* that:

> . . . *there grew within me the conviction that as never before in a war between many nations the forces that stood for human good and men's rights were this time confronted by a completely evil conspiracy [of Hitler and his allies]. Because only by the utter destruction of the Axis [Germany and its then-ally Italy] was a decent world possible, the war became for me a crusade.*

Ike's success in North Africa made him world-famous. In December 1943, President Roosevelt met in Cairo, Egypt, with Prime Minister Churchill, and they agreed that it was time for the invasion of Europe. Ike was called back to London to become supreme commander of the Allied Expeditionary Force to plan and carry out that invasion. He then returned to work on his earlier plan for the invasion of Europe by sea from England to France.

Taking charge of Operation Overlord was the greatest challenge of Eisenhower's career. It called for the largest combined air-sea-and-land operation in military history, and he would have to draw up its plan, down to the last detail.

The problems were many and did not involve just the logistics of waging war. First Ike had to gain the cooperation of the political and military leaders of Great Britain. Then too, he had to win the cooperation of the leaders of the American military. The Allied air forces wanted to bomb inside Germany. Ike disagreed and insisted that Allied air power should instead bomb targets in France, to make the invasion easier. He was so set on this that he threatened to resign if he did not win this point of strategy. He did win in the end, and bombing raids that took out railroad lines and bridges near Normandy paved the way for D-Day, the name given to that day on which the invasion of Normandy, France, was to begin.

On the morning of June 6, 1944, a few moments after the invasion had begun, a radio correspondent asked Ike if he was not nervous about the campaign.

"Nervous?" Ike replied. "I'm so nervous I'm boiling over inside."

But he didn't look nervous. Outwardly, he was his usually calm, self-assured self, confident in the success of the mission. He had planned for it for two years. Just for good luck, though, he carried with him three coins—American, British, and French.

The Allied invasion was led by thousands of parachutists leaping from C-47 transport planes. Many would serve as infantrymen behind enemy lines, while others were engineers who would attempt to seize German airfields or, failing that, build new landing strips for Allied planes to land on.

Over 900 tow planes and gliders set down a second wave of assault troops inland for the battle of Normandy. More than 3,000 tanks, jeeps, and other military vehicles, and more than 2.8 million ship-tons of supplies including artillery pieces and great barrels of gasoline were soon brought ashore.

While Allied naval guns and bombers assaulted the Normandy beach fortifications, the infantry swarmed ashore. Five beachheads were established in all. The Americans came ashore at Omaha Beach and Utah Beach. Omaha was the scene of the fiercest fighting.

As tense hours passed and the invasion was in full force, radio broadcasts announced that many Allied troops had landed near Caen, 65 miles southeast of Cherbourg, France. A German communique put them at the mouth of the Seine River.

That night and next day, a third and fourth wave of Allied forces would have an even tougher time securing the five strategic beachheads in Eisenhower's invasion plan. By then, German generals had learned of the invasion and brought their own forces to bear on the Allies.

Ike had already won what he most hoped to gain: The Nazis had been taken by surprise. They had not known when or where the invasion would take place and had been caught completely unaware. The cost of the Normandy invasion was 73,000 American dead and wounded and 49,000 British and Canadian casualties.

Now the Allies had a foothold in Europe, but more decisions on tactics and strategy would have to be made before the Nazis could be beaten. Again, Eisenhower was the man to make them. Two months after the invasion, he went to Normandy to confer with General Omar Bradley, commander of the U.S. Twelfth Army Group. The Germans were at the east, south, and west, keeping the Allies from advancing far from the beachheads they had won. Eisenhower decided the time was right for an offensive to break out across France. The tactic was bold, but it worked. By December, Paris and most of France was liberated.

General Dwight D. Eisenhower stops during an inspection of rear-line supply facilities at Cherbourg, France, to ask T/5 William Carpenter of Nashville, Tenn., how his ammunition handling crew is getting along.
(U.S. Army Military History Institute)

The German industrial heartland, the Ruhr Valley, was next on Ike's list of targets. But before Allied troops could cross the Rhine River onto German soil, the Nazis began a counteroffensive in the Ardennes region of Belgium on December 14. It became known as the Battle of the Bulge, one of the biggest and most decisive battles of the war.

Some Allied leaders thought the Nazi offensive was a small, local battle, but Eisenhower thought otherwise. He believed it was the start of a major campaign by the German High Command, a last-ditch effort to stop the Allies, and ordered a proper defense.

The Germans had penetrated deep into Belgium, creating a dent, or "bulge," in the Allied lines. At the same time, the main Allied supply port of Antwerp, Belgium, was suffering from intensive V-2 rocket bombardment. An American force, though surrounded and outnumbered, bravely held out at Bastogne. The U.S. First and Ninth armies attacked the Germans from the north while General Patton and his Third Army attacked from the south. The Germans were destroyed or routed by January 16, 1945, but not without some 77,000 Allied casualties.

Fortunately, Eisenhower's correct instinct about the German counteroffensive had been put into action, and a major counterattack saved the Allies from suffering heavier casualties and losing vital ground. Though more battles followed, the Battle of the Bulge has come to be known as Hitler's last offensive.

Eisenhower's next major decision was for the Allies to fight a decisive battle west of the Rhine. Not gambling on the Nazis to be too weak in manpower and firepower to resist, he ordered a full-scale attack. This decision caused him to make a choice for which he was later criticized. By focusing on crossing the Rhine, he left it to the Soviet Army to take Berlin and gain a political foothold there.

More major battles were fought in the following months as Allied armored divisions advanced to the Rhine River in Germany and cleared most of France and Belgium of German forces. Allied forces under General Bradley and British Field Marshal Bernard Montgomery smashed through the strongly fortified Siegfried Line, crossed the Rhine, and overran western Germany. After Western and Russian armies were victorious over the Nazis at Torgau in Saxony, German resistance collapsed and an unconditional surrender came on May 7, 1945.

General Eisenhower was honored with the highest awards of his own country and those of Great Britain, France, and the Soviet Union, most of them given to an American for the first time. Although he never commanded troops in the field, Ike emerged from the war as its greatest hero. He returned to a hero's welcome in Washington and accepted it humbly on behalf of the Americans who had fought under him. Appearing before a joint session of Congress, he said,

My imagination cannot picture a more dramatic moment than this in the life of an American. I stand here in the presence of the elected federal lawmakers of our great Republic, the very core of our American political life and a symbol of those things that we call the American heritage. To preserve that heritage, more than three million of our citizens, at your behest, resolutely faced every terror the ruthless Nazi could devise. I am summoned before you as the representative—the commander— of those three million American men and women to whom you desire to pay America's tribute for military victory.

In humble realization that they who earned your commendation should properly be here to receive it, I am nevertheless proud and honored to serve as your agent in conveying it to them. I have seen the American proved on battlegrounds of Africa and Europe over which armies have been fighting for two thousand years of recorded history. None of those battlefields has seen a more worthy soldier than the trained American . . .

The battle front and the home front, together we have found the victory! But even the banners of victory cannot hide from our sight the sacrifices in which victory has been bought. The hard task of a commander is to send men into battle knowing some of them—often many—must be killed or wounded in order that necessary missions may be achieved.

It is a soul-killing task; my sorrow is not only for the fine young lives lost or broken, but it is equally for the parents, the wives, and the friends who have been bereaved. The blackness of their grief can be relieved only by the faith that all this shall not happen again!

A special train bore him into Kansas a few days later, and he returned home to Abilene and another hero's welcome.

Eisenhower was soon thereafter promoted to five-star general, and sent to Germany to command the occupation forces. In November 1945 he became chief of staff of the U.S. Army, but three years later he resigned and began a new life as a civilian, as president of Columbia University in New York City.

Ike took a leave of absence from Columbia in 1950 to become supreme commander of the Allied Powers in Europe. After organizing the defense forces in the North Atlantic Treaty Organization (NATO) in 1952, and still riding his popularity from the war, he became a Republican candidate for president. With millions shouting "I like Ike!" he easily defeated his Democratic opponent, Senator Adlai E. Stevenson of Illinois, and on January 20, 1953, became the 34th president of the United States.

After serving two terms as president, Eisenhower resumed his life as a civilian in 1960. His robust 175-pound, five-foot ten-inch frame often could be seen on the golf course with friends, politicians, and celebrities.

Eisenhower died at the age of 78 on March 28, 1969, after a long fight against heart disease.

In his eulogy of Eisenhower, President Richard Nixon said, "He was both a great and good man. To millions the world over he was a symbol of decency and hope . . . As long as free men cherish their freedom, Dwight Eisenhower will stand with them, as he stood during war and peace; strong, confident, and courageous."

Eisenhower's biographer, Stephen E. Ambrose, said of him in his biography, *Eisenhower:*

Ike was a great leader, but did not get the opportunity to prove he was a great soldier. His greatest trait may have been that his fellow military leaders and his men trusted him—from [Great Britain's Prime Minister Winston] Churchill to the buck private in the army, to [France's General Charles] de Gaulle, people trusted Ike.

[Great Britain's] Field Marshal [Bernard] Montgomery once declared, "I would not class Ike as a great soldier in the true sense

of the word. His real strength lies in his human qualities. He has the power of drawing the hearts of men towards him as a magnet attracts a bit of metal. He merely has to smile at you, and you trust him at once."

While he was president, Eisenhower assembled some artifacts of his life and wrote two documents. He put these in a copper box and buried them inside one of the brick chimneys of his farmhouse at Gettysburg, now a National Historic site. He left instructions that the box is not to be opened until well into the 21st century.

It is not known what the documents contain, but some believe that in one of them, Eisenhower reveals his true opinions of the Allied officers who served under him in World War II. The other apparently is a message to the American people, with his views on the future of politics in the United States and the world.

When his time capsule is finally opened, we may know what the quiet-spoken general and president could not tell us when he was alive.

Chronology

October 14, 1890	born in Denison, Texas
1915	graduated from West Point; assigned to Fort Sam Houston, Texas
July 1, 1916	marries Mamie Geneva Doud
1917–29	serves at army bases in U.S. and abroad
1929	assigned to Washington, D.C., office of assistant secretary of war
1932	assistant to General Douglas MacArthur
1935–39	serves under MacArthur in Philippines
1939	appointed to general staff of U.S. War Department
1942	commander of Allied invasion of North Africa
1944	named Supreme Commander, Allied Expeditionary Force
1945–48	chief of staff of U.S. Army
1948–50	president of Columbia University
1951–53	commander of NATO forces in Europe
1953–61	34th president of the United States
March 28, 1969	dies in Washington, D.C.

Further Reading

Books by Dwight D. Eisenhower
Crusade in Europe. Garden City, N.Y.: Doubleday, 1948. Eisenhower's own account of World War II in Europe.

The Eisenhower Diaries, ed. Robert Ferrell. New York: Norton, 1981. Eisenhower's diaries of his life and the war.

Books About Dwight D. Eisenhower
Ambrose, Stephen E. *Eisenhower.* New York: Simon & Schuster, 1983. A very complete biography, emphasis on World War II.

Beschloss, Michael. *Eisenhower, A Centennial Life.* New York: HarperCollins, 1990. Highlights of Ike's life with many pictures.

Cannon, Marian. *Dwight D. Eisenhower.* New York: Watts, 1990. Good young adult biography of war years and Ike's presidency.

Davis, Kenneth S. *Soldier of Democracy.* Garden City, N.Y.: Doubleday, 1945. Very readable biography of his life, especially in World War II.

Ellis, Rafaela. *Dwight D. Eisenhower.* Ada, Okla.: Garrett Educational Corp., 1989. Good young adult biography.

Jacqueline Cochran
(1910–1980)
Director, Women's Air Force
Service Pilots

Jacqueline Cochran, director of Women's Air Force Service Pilots, 1941–1945.
(Courtesy National Air and Space Museum, Smithsonian Institution)

*M*any American women served bravely and in roles of leadership in World War II. Some were nurses, others served in the women's auxiliary units of the armed forces. Oveta Culp Hobby was the first director of the Women's Army Corps (WACs), in which about 100,000 women served as medical technicians, clerks, and secretaries, relieving soldiers of noncombat duty in World War II. Mildred Helen McAfee commanded the WAVES (Women Appointed for Voluntary Emergency Service), the naval counterpart of the WACs. Eighty thousand women served in communications, air traffic control, naval air navigation, and clerical positions during World War II, relieving male naval personnel for sea duty. Another 10,000 women served in the women's reserve of the U.S. Coast Guard, called the SPARS (from the motto "Semper Paratus," meaning "always prepared").

Jacqueline Cochran organized and directed the WASPs, the Women's Airforce Service Pilots, during the war. From her humble beginnings, no one would have guessed that she would become one of America's best pilots, or that she would play a leadership role in World War II.

Cochran was born in Pensacola, Florida, in 1910. She was orphaned at an early age and never knew the exact date of her birth. She lived with poor foster parents in the sawmill camp towns of Florida and Georgia.

"Until I was eight years old, I had no shoes," she wrote in her autobiography, *The Stars at Noon*. "My bed was usually a pallet on the floor and sometimes just the floor. My dresses in the first seven years of my life were usually made from cast-off flour sacks."

At the age of eight, she went to work in the cotton mills of Columbus, Georgia, earning six cents an hour working the 12-hour night shift. It was hard work for long hours, but she was happy because she was able to buy her first pair of shoes. In her spare time, she read.

After several years, when the millworkers went on strike, she found work in a beauty shop. Later she moved to Montgomery, Alabama, and worked in the beauty shop of a department store. In her teens, she bought a Model T Ford and learned auto mechanics so she could maintain the car herself.

Cochran then became interested in nursing. After three years of training, she worked as a nurse in several towns in northern Florida. Before long, she moved to Pensacola, Florida, and returned to beauty shop work. After about a year, she went to New York City and worked for the famous beautician, Antoine, at his Saks-Fifth Avenue salon. Soon she spent her winters working at his second salon in Miami Beach, Florida.

At a party in Miami in 1932, she met Floyd Bostwick Odlum, a banker and industrialist. She told him she would like to work for a big cosmetics company, selling beauty aids to stores across the country. She thought it would be fun to travel from store to store and help the company grow.

"You would need wings to do all that!" Odlum told her.

The suggestion changed her life. Cochran decided to spend her three weeks' vacation learning how to fly a plane. The instructor said it usually took two to three months to get a pilot's license, but Cochran learned to handle a plane quickly at Roosevelt Field on Long Island, New York. After only three days of instruction, she flew her first solo flight.

It wasn't an easy solo. The plane's engine stopped in mid-flight, but Cochran managed to glide the plane down safely for a "dead-stick landing." Cochran did not let the scare deter her. She stayed with her training and received her pilot's license even before her vacation was over.

In *Four Women of Courage,* biographer Bennett Wayne says one of Cochran's fellow aviators, Captain Kenneth P. Behr, said of her: "We couldn't help rooting for Jackie. Here she was, a pretty blonde who hadn't even finished grammar school, but she buckled down over the heavy textbooks and mastered celestial navigation and Morse Code."

She still had vacation time left to rent a plane and fly to Montreal, Canada, to attend an air meet of sportsmen pilots.

"Flying was now in my blood," she later recalled in her book.

Cochran resigned her job as a beautician and drove to San Diego, California, where she took extra courses at a flying school. After that, she bought an old Travelair plane for $1,200, and earned a commercial pilot's license.

There were few women pilots in the early 1930s, but Cochran was determined to be one of the best. She trained more and by 1934 was considered a skilled pilot. That same year, she started a cosmetics firm that grew and prospered under her management. Soon she was flying all over the country to expand her own business.

Deciding it was time to enter her first air race, she became the only American woman to enter the McRobertson London-Melbourne (Australia) air race in 1934. It was a major international event put on by manufacturers to test their new planes. A friend, Wesley Smith, agreed to be her copilot.

The race was to start in London and end in Melbourne. But the American Gee Bee racing plane Cochran and Smith were to fly wasn't completely built yet. They took it by ship to England, and mechanics worked on it during the ocean crossing. After some scary trial flights, they started the race, but the plane didn't feel right to Cochran. Later, after nearly crash-landing over Europe, she and Smith decided to drop out of the race because the plane was too unsafe to fly any farther. It was a wise decision. Gee Bees were fast but small and unstable planes that were notoriously dangerous. Many pilots lost their lives racing them.

In 1935, Cochran became the first woman to enter the Bendix Transcontinental Air Race, from Los Angeles to Cleveland, Ohio. Officials told her it was too difficult for a woman, but she got signatures on a letter from all the male pilots saying it was okay with them if she wanted to enter the race.

On the night of the takeoff, fog rolled off the ocean so heavy that pilots could not see the end of the runway. The plane ahead of Cochran's crashed on takeoff and the pilot was killed. The owner of the Northrop Gamma plane, which Cochran was to fly, begged her to call off the flight, but she believed she could use the plane's instruments to take it up.

She began her blind takeoff, but as the plane moved down the runway, its engine did not seem to be building up enough power. Just before the plane was about to crash into a fence at the end of the runway, its wheels left the ground. But the radio antenna had caught on the fence and was pulled off. Cochran had no radio to navigate or communicate with, but had made it up into the sky.

Hours later, approaching the Grand Canyon, Cochran saw that an electrical storm was building up. At the same time, she noticed her plane was overheated. The winds were very strong, it began to rain, and lightning flashed all about her. She feared she could not fly the overheated plane safely through the storm so she reluctantly flew to the nearest airport. She hadn't finished the race, but had proved that a woman could enter the Bendix.

Cochran and Floyd Odlum were married in 1936. She nearly lost her life in several flying accidents, but he knew how much she loved flying and encouraged her to continue. Trying the Bendix Race again in 1937, she came in third.

"It's the number on your plane," other pilots told her about her bad luck. Her plane's number was 13. But Cochran laughed. She wasn't superstititous and, in fact, thought the number would bring her good luck some day.

She entered the Bendix again in 1938, piloting a small Seversky pursuit plane that she had never flown before. Again, she encountered trouble. Soon after taking the plane up, the gas tank in the right wing became blocked, and she could get enough fuel only if she tipped the plane. But she managed to win the race anyway, and the cheers of thousands at the finish and the admiration of pilots everywhere.

Cochran became one of the most famous women pilots in America, entering more races and testing new planes, engines, fuels, instruments, and propellers. Some of these failed and nearly cost her her life, but she kept on flying and testing products.

As her cosmetics business prospered during the mid-1930s, she bought a home and a 600-acre date farm in the California desert near Indio, where she and her husband spent most of their time when she wasn't flying. Also during these years, Jacqueline Cochran and Amelia Earhart, then the most famous American woman flier, became close friends. Earhart had been the first woman to cross the Atlantic by airplane, in 1928, and the first woman to make a solo flight across the Atlantic, in 1932.

In 1937, Earhart and copilot Fred Noonan were to attempt to fly around the world. She spent most of the last few months before the flight resting at the Cochran ranch in California. Cochran had doubts about the success of the flight, sensing it might end disastrously.

Earhart and Noonan's plane was lost over the Pacific between New Guinea and Howland Island. Their fate remains a mystery to this day. Some believe the Pacific leg of their flight was in part a mission requested by President Roosevelt, to spy on Japanese military activity in the area. If they had survived a crash-landing, they may have been executed as spies. Cochran was among the many pilots who searched the Pacific without finding any sign of her friend or her plane.

As the Nazi encroachment on Europe extended in the late 1930s, Cochran became certain that women pilots would be needed in the war. At a luncheon early in 1941 in Washington, D.C., she told Henry H. "Hap" Arnold, chief of the Army Air Corps, she wished she could do something to help in the war effort. America was not yet in the war in Europe, but England had been at war with Germany since 1939, after Germany invaded and occupied Poland.

Arnold told her about the men who were flying American-built planes from Canada to England for use by Britain's Royal Air Force. In her autobiography, Cochran says he suggested, "Why don't you fly one of the bombers over to England? We need every plane we can get over there, and besides, your flying would call attention to the need."

Cochran thought the job was just right for her. But she ran into trouble being accepted by some of the male pilots. One stole equipment out of her cockpit just before she could take her first test flight for the mission. Some others threatened to go on strike if she flew the plane, but a compromise was reached when Cochran agreed to let a male pilot take the plane up and land it, but she would take over the controls while it was in the air.

This was how Cochran flew her first bomber to England, in June of 1941. Nearly at daybreak, after an overnight flight, tracer bullets shot up around the plane as Cochran piloted it over the ocean, nearing the coast of Ireland. At first, the plane had been mistaken as an enemy aircraft, but then the firing stopped. Twelve hours after takeoff, the plane reached Scotland. Newspapers everywhere told the story and called Cochran "the glamour girl of aviation."

After she returned to the United States a few days later, President Franklin D. Roosevelt invited Cochran to the White House for lunch. She told him about the "Battle of Britain" the English military and civilians were waging, bravely withstanding the devastating German air bombings of British cities.

Two days later, General Arnold summoned Cochran to his office. She says in her autobiography: "An English official has asked me if you would organize a group of American women pilots and take them to England," he told her. He said that England needed experienced women pilots to fly planes to relieve male pilots of domestic duties so they could fly in combat.

Cochran accepted the job and flew all over America gathering women pilots willing to fly for England. Twenty-five were chosen and trained, and Cochran took them to England, in charge as flight captain.

Cochran and the other women pilots learned to fly military planes in wartime England. They flew both combat and support planes from factories to airports and from one airport to another, transporting people, equipment, and supplies.

Cochran remained in charge of the women pilots program in England until shortly after the United States entered the war in December 1941. Then she got a brief message from General Arnold: "Come home."

Back in Washington, Cochran was asked by Arnold to find more women pilots and organize a training program for them. She would be put in charge of an operation in America similar to the one she had organized in England, so women pilots could relieve American male pilots of noncombat duty and free them for action.

Cochran accepted and chose Houston, Texas, as the training base for the Army Air Force's new women's auxiliary. She started with a new group of 25 volunteers and after several months of directing their training, the women pilots were ready to graduate.

But Cochran was ill at her ranch in California. She could hardly stand up, the result of injuries suffered earlier while testing planes. The nearest airport where she could take a plane to Houston was 200 miles away, in Phoenix, Arizona, but her doctor insisted she could not sit up in a car to take her there.

Determined to be at her first class's graduation, Cochran thought of a way to make the trip to Phoenix while lying flat on her back. She hired a hearse. It took her to the airport in Phoenix, and she got to Houston in time to personally hand out each diploma.

Soon as she was well again, Cochran resumed her post as director of the WASPs—the Women's Air Force Service Pilots. Before long, dozens of similar groups of women fliers were in training at other air fields where she had set up programs.

When two women pilots were killed when their planes crashed in North Carolina, Cochran flew there to give courage and solace to some of the others who were afraid to complete training. When they said the planes weren't safe, Cochran personally flew each of the planes, giving them all a hard flight test. Each had something wrong with it, but she told the women that no plane in wartime was perfectly safe. The women returned to their planes, but a few days later another plane crashed. The pilot lived but suffered a skull fracture.

Cochran was determined to learn the cause of the plane crashes. She discovered that sugar had been put in the gasoline so the engine stopped shortly after the plane would take off. An enemy agent had done it, to sabotage the program.

With Cochran's leadership, before the war ended, 1,830 women had taken the flight training course and 1,074 of them graduated, flying about 60 million miles and relieving American pilots of noncombat duty. Thirty-eight WASP pilots were killed in flight accidents during the war. Cochran was awarded the Distinguished Service Medal for her work.

Also during the war, Cochran was a foreign correspondent for *Liberty* magazine in the Pacific. Later she reported the Japanese surrender and, back in Europe, covered the Nuremberg war crimes trials of Nazi officials.

Returning home, Cochran resumed management of her cosmetics business and tested planes and entered air races again. She also became interested in politics. In 1952 she flew to Paris to show former General Dwight D. Eisenhower a two-hour film of a rally in New York's Madison Square Garden at which 15,000 people shouted, "We want Ike! We want Ike!" Cochran's effort is credited with helping Eisenhower decide to run for president.

Meanwhile, the jet air age had begun and Cochran wanted to be a part of it. In 1952 she became a flight consultant for a Canadian company building the F-86 Sabre Jet and made speed tests of the plane at Edwards Air Force Base in California. There she met Colonel Charles "Chuck" Yeager, the first person to fly a plane faster than the speed of sound.

Yeager helped Cochran learn more about flying at faster speeds and higher altitudes. Though often in poor health, she continued to fly and set new world speed records.

On May 18, 1953, flying her F-86 Sabre Jet at a speed of over 760 miles an hour over the desert in California, Cochran became the first woman to pilot a plane faster than the speed of sound. She was awarded the International Flying Organization's gold medal for outstanding accomplishment by any pilot, man or woman, during that year.

In the following years, Cochran set more than 200 flying records, including the fastest speed flown by a woman (1,429 miles per hour) in 1964. She also was honored with the Legion of Merit and the Distinguished Flying Cross.

Jacqueline Cochran became the first woman to land a jet on an aircraft carrier; the first woman to fly at Mach 2, twice the

Jacqueline Cochran becomes first woman to fly a plane faster than the speed of sound, in 1953.
(Courtesy of National Air and Space Museum, Smithsonian Institution)

speed of sound; and the first woman to pilot a jet across the Atlantic. She retired with the rank of colonel in the Air Force Reserve in 1970.

In the preface to her book, her husband wrote:

> *I have said many times that Jackie is fearless, and yet she runs wildly from a snake, and I have seen her almost hysterical from listening to a good old-fashioned ghost story. However, I have never seen her back away from real danger. Certain it is that she is fearless of death and equally certain it is that she considers a barrier only something to surmount.*

Cochran herself wrote in her autobiography: "Earthbound souls know only the underside of the atmosphere in which they live. But go up higher—above the dust and water vapor—and the sky turns dark until one can see the stars at noon. I have."

Jacqueline Cochran, who also worked tirelessly on behalf of the Camp Fire Girls and for education for needy children, died at her ranch in Indio, California, on August 9, 1980.

In *Four Women of Courage,* Wayne Bennett reported that, in tribute to her, Chuck Yeager said:

> *"Jackie and I had one experience that can never be duplicated. I as the first man to pass the sonic barrier and Jackie as the first woman to do so each took a Sabre-jet, climbed to nearly fifty thousand feet of altitude and put the two planes, almost wing tip to wing tip, into a full-power vertical dive past the barrier, as a sort of supersonic duet.*
>
> *"I salute Jacqueline Cochran as a good pilot and a fine person who has often had to accomplish things the hard way. Her many contributions to the progress of aviation have helped make our world a better and safer place in which to live."*

Chronology

1910	born in Pensacola, Florida
1918	while living with foster parents in Georgia, she works in cotton mills
1924	leaves home; works in a beauty shop in Montgomery, Alabama
1927	completes three years of nurse training and nurses the poor in Florida
1930	moves to New York City; works in beauty shop
1932	takes flying lessons and gets pilot's license
1935	first woman to enter Bendix Transcontinental Air Race
1936	marries industrialist Floyd B. Odlum
1937	takes third place in Bendix race
1938	wins first place in Bendix race
1939	sets speed record flying from Burbank to San Mateo, California, and back at 309 mph
1941	flys bomber to London; starts British Air Transport Auxiliary
1941–45	director of WASPs, Women's Air Force Service Pilots
1953	first woman to fly a plane faster than the speed of sound
1954	autobiography, *The Stars at Noon*, published

1960	first woman to fly at Mach 2, twice the speed of sound, and to land a jet on an aircraft carrier
1961	sets altitude record of 55,253 feet
1962	first woman to fly a jet plane across the Atlantic Ocean
1964	sets women's world speed record of 1,429 miles per hour
1970	retires as colonel in Air Force Reserve
August 9, 1980	dies at her ranch in Indio, California

Further Reading

Book by Jacqueline Cochran
The Stars at Noon. Boston: Little, Brown, 1954. Jacqueline Cochran's exciting autobiography, the definitive account of her life.

Book About Jacqueline Cochran
Wayne, Bennett. *Four Women of Courage.* Champaign, Ill.: Garrard Publishing Co., 1975. A chapter with a good summary of Cochran's life and career.

Article About Jacqueline Cochran
Current Biography, 1963. New York: H.W. Wilson, 1963. Biography of Cochran up to 1963.

General Omar Bradley
(1893–1981)
Commander, Second Army
and Twelfth Army Corps

*General Omar N. Bradley, chairman of the Joint
Chiefs of Staff, 1950.*
(U.S. Army Military History Institute)

*H*e had clashed with British Field Marshal Sir Bernard Montgomery, as had other American generals, and his relationship
with General Dwight D. Eisenhower, while friendly, was never
especially warm. But General Omar Bradley, one of the greatest American military leaders of World War II, was always

popular with his troops. Their nickname for him, the "GI's general," meant they considered him a leader but also a soldier, like themselves. He proved to be both as he led more than half a million troops to victory over a German counteroffensive and established the first Allied linkup with the Soviet Army.

A West Point-educated "book general," Bradley regarded war as a series of mathematical problems, to be approached, he said, "slow and sure. Never use intuition."

Omar Nelson Bradley was born February 12, 1893, in Clark, Missouri. His father named him Omar, after an editor friend, and Nelson, after a local doctor. As a boy, Omar loved to hike and hunt with an air rifle on trips with his father, a country school teacher. His father died when Omar was 14, and his mother took in sewing to support them.

During high school, Omar worked as a laborer in the boiler repair shops of the Wabash Railroad. After graduation and with the help of his congressman, Bradley won an appointment to West Point in 1911. He was a good student and cadet while at the Academy. He was also an athlete, winning letters in both baseball and football.

Upon graduation from the Military Academy in 1915, he was appointed a 2nd lieutenant and assigned to the 14th Infantry at Fort George G. Wright in Washington. The following year he accompanied his regiment to Arizona for border duty, was promoted to 1st lieutenant, and married his high school sweetheart, Mary Elizabeth Quayle. She accompanied him, over the years, to 28 different posts.

Bradley did not serve overseas during World War I, but won steady promotion for stateside duty in the West and Midwest. He attained the rank of major in 1920, and was assigned to West Point where he served as an instructor in mathematics for four years. After advanced studies at the Infantry School at Fort Benning, Georgia, in 1925 he was ordered to duty with the infantry at Schofield Barracks in Hawaii. He remained there with the 29th Infantry until May 1928, serving his final year in

Hawaii in charge of National Guard and Reserve Affairs for the Hawaiian Department.

Returning to the United States, Bradley spent a year studying at the Command and General Staff School at Fort Leavenworth, Kansas, graduating in 1929. For the next four years, he served as an instructor at the Infantry School at Fort Benning, Georgia, and was in charge of the weapons section. Afterward he attended the Army War College at Carlisle Barracks, Pennsylvania, and was graduated in June 1934. He then became an instructor in tactics at West Point and in 1936 was promoted to lieutenant colonel. The next year he became plans and training officer at the academy until June 1938, when he was called to Washington, D.C., for duty on the War Department general staff as assistant secretary.

As war spread in Europe and the United States prepared for possible entry into it, in February 1941 Bradley was assigned again to the Infantry School at Fort Benning, this time as commandant. At the age of 48, he became the first of his 1915 West Point class to be appointed to brigadier general.

Shortly after the United States entered World War II, Bradley was promoted to major general and assigned as commanding general of the 82nd Infantry Division at Camp Claiborne, Louisiana. In June 1942, he became commanding general of the 28th Infantry Division at Camp Livingston, Lousiana. Bradley displayed great physical endurance in army maneuvers, running through obstacle courses and swinging across ravines and streams or dangling from ropes while much younger soldiers couldn't keep up with him.

In February 1943, Bradley was posted overseas and sent to North Africa. In *Bradley: A Soldier's Story,* he says that after arriving there, he wrote his wife, who could not go along this time because of war restrictions, "It is an interesting assignment. Only temporary, but I hope to make it permanent."

Bradley's first assignment in North Africa was as field aide to General Eisenhower. They had played football on the same team at West Point, and Eisenhower was impressed by

Bradley's calm confidence, professional proficiency, and low-key manner.

In his biography, *Eisenhower,* Stephen Ambrose writes that Ike knew he could count on Bradley, and said of him, "This officer is about the best-rounded, well-balanced senior officer that we have in the service. His judgments are always sound. He is respected by British and Americans alike. I feel there is no position in the army that he could not fill with success."

Eisenhower assigned Bradley to be his "eyes and ears" in Africa. Bradley fulfilled that role by making long and dangerous reconnaissance trips by plane or jeep.

On April 16, 1943, the battle moved into the northern hills of Tunisia. Eisenhower named Bradley commander of the U.S. 2nd Corps in North Africa, which began making its way to Bizerte. Bradley succeeded General George S. Patton because Patton was primarily a tank expert and the new zone of operations was mainly an infantry fight.

Under Bradley, the infantry smashed through a German minefield to take strategic Hill 609. On May 7, the Americans with the British 1st and 8th armies captured Bizerte and Tunis, cutting the enemy forces in Tunisia in two. Fanning out from the two cities, they then bore down relentlessly upon the Germans and Italians wherever the enemy troops attempted to make a stand. Finally, on the morning of May 9, Major General Fritz Krause, German artillery commander in the Afrika Korps, sent word to Bradley requesting an armistice for the purpose of negotiating the surrender of the German forces.

Bradley demanded that the surrender be both unconditional and prompt, and that the Germans must immediately cease to destroy their war equipment. Krause accepted the terms, and more than 40,000 thoroughly beaten German soldiers surrendered.

The next day, Bradley's general order to his officers and men was: "This ends operations for the American Second Corps in North Africa."

Biographer Stephen Ambrose says Bradley received the following message from the British commander, General Sir

Harold Alexander: "Well done, indeed. I and all the 18th Army Group are delighted at your wonderful success in the north, culminating in the capture of Bizerte. Your Corps has played a major part in this great victory, and I wish to express to every single officer and man you command my gratitude and thanks."

Bradley proved that even war fought on a desert plain under the harshest circumstances could and should be waged by tactics taught at the Infantry School. His military tactics were summed up by one of his pet sayings, "Hit the enemy twice: first, to find out what he's got; then, to take it away from him."

The day after the collapse of the enemy in Tunisia, Bradley was on his way to Algiers to help plan the invasion of Sicily, again as commander of the U.S. 2nd Corps, and to be commissioned as a (three-star) lieutenant general. On July 10, Bradley, with just his aide and jeep driver, waded ashore to reconnoiter that dangerous enemy-held island west of Italy's "boot."

In Sicily, Bradley rode in a jeep from six to eight hours a day, saying the bumpy ride was good for the liver.

Ernie Pyle, the popular war correspondent who spent some time with Bradley in Sicily, reported frequently about the general's heroics during August 1943. In his syndicated newspaper column, Pyle wrote that "Bradley insisted on keeping his command post up close, sometimes distressingly close, behind the front lines."

Bradley was popular himself, with general officers who called him "Brad" on informal occasions, and with those who served under him and called him the fairest man they'd ever known. Though often appearing to be easygoing, mild, and polite, he insisted that those under his command either deliver the goods or they would be replaced.

During the Sicily campaign, Bradley lived in and operated out of an army truck fixed up like a tourist trailer, sitting alone many nights for hours studying maps of the country and planning out strategies for the next day.

One day Bradley and Pyle were lunching with Major General Terry Allen at his 1st Infantry Division command post, an old building close to the front. Just outside was a battery of big guns that blasted away while the three ate. The noise was deafening and the building shook so that tables and dishes jumped and blasts seemed to sweep through the room. Bradley casually said to Allen, "Terry, could you arrange to have those guns shoot over the building instead of through it?"

In November 1943, rumors spread that Bradley would probably be named to head the American field forces in the anticipated western invasion of Europe. When General George C. Marshall asked General Eisenhower who should command the American army group in the attack across the English Channel, Ike replied, "You should take Bradley. He has never caused me one moment of worry."

Bradley was summoned to England less than a week later, to help plan the largest invasion in history. He spent the remainder of 1943 and the winter and spring of 1944 preparing his First Army for the Normandy landings.

It was feared that the Allies would suffer heavy casualties in the invasion of Europe, but Bradley, according to biographer Ambrose, told fellow American officers, "When the time comes, you will be surprised by the naval gunfire and air power we have. Some of you won't come back, but it will be very few. In the Tunisian campaign, we lost an average of three or four men to one thousand, and certainly seeing a show like this ought to be worth that chance."

But Bradley knew that ultimate victory in war could come at a high cost in American lives. In his autobiography, *Bradley: A Soldier's Story,* he wrote,

> *In time of war the only value that can be affixed to any unit is the tactical value of that unit in winning the war. Even the lives of those men assigned to it become nothing more than tools to be used in the accomplishment of that mission. War has neither the time nor heart to concern itself with the individual and the dignity of man. Men must be subordinated to the effort that comes with fighting a war, and as a consequence men must die that objectives might be taken. For a commander the agony of war is not in its dangers, deprivations, or the fear of defeat but in the knowledge*

that with each new day men's lives must be spent to pay the costs of that day's objectives.

Bradley made frequent pre-invasion visits to airfields in England. On one inspection, he saw a soldier awkwardly charging with fixed bayonet in a practice session, and nudged him off-balance. After showing the proper way to execute the assault maneuver, he apologized, saying, "I didn't mean to treat you rough."

It was typical of Bradley's politeness and humility. When making a phone call, he would say "if you please" to the army operator or "thank you" to the driver who pulled his army truck out of the way so Bradley's jeep could pass.

To bolster morale among his troops, Bradley told them during invasion training in England, "I will see you on the beaches." When the dawn of D-Day arrived, June 6, 1944, he did just that, wading ashore with them from the cruiser *Augusta* and, under heavy enemy gunfire, scaling the cliffs near Omaha beach along the Normandy coast.

Four weeks of heavy fighting followed, during which the Allies were able to advance only 30 miles into France. Eisenhower needed a general to lead the GIs in the battles to follow. Again he chose Bradley. Seven weeks after the Normandy landings, Bradley and his troops smashed through the German lines at St. Lo and opened the way through Avranches for the liberation of France.

Bradley turned over command of the First Army on August 1 to General Courtney Hughes and assumed overall command of the American ground forces of the huge Twelfth Army Group, which was made up of the U.S. First, Third, Ninth, and Fifteenth armies. Over half a million men would be needed to reclaim France from the Germans.

Bradley often tried to out-think the enemy generals in strategy. That December, as snow began falling over the Ardennes—the "Western Front" of the First World War—he studied the German positions around Luxembourg and decided that the Germans might very well try to break through the American lines. Field Marshal Karl von Rundstedt did just that a few days later in a last-ditch effort to keep back the Allies. Bradley was ready, and his army broke the back of the German offensive in the Battle of the Bulge.

In early 1945, Bradley won promotion to four-star general, and the Allies crossed the Rhine River, smashed through the strongly fortified Siegfried Line, and overran western Germany.

As the war in Europe was winding down, Bradley volunteered to go to the Pacific and help end the war with the Japanese. But to do so would have meant taking a subordinate role to General Douglas MacArthur who was supreme Allied commander there. Eisenhower persuaded Bradley that he did not need to take a demotion, and General Marshall withdrew consideration of sending Bradley to the Pacific.

Bradley wrote in his autobiography, "I was a soldier. We had defeated one enemy, but from our distance, Japan still loomed large. [Generals] Hodge, Patton, Simpson —a great many of us—were eager to join in the final conquest of Japan. No U.S. soldier had commanded large Army forces against both Germany and Japan. It would have been an unusual, if not unique, honor. But Ike was right in his assessment. I did not want to go to the Pacific in any job lower than army group commander."

After the historic meeting of the Western and Russian armies at Torgau in Saxony, the German Army collapsed, and an unconditional surrender was signed at Rheims on May 7.

Bradley had many thoughts and feelings then, as he wrote in his autobiography:

"The war against Germany was over. The Third Reich lay pulverized beyond recognition. It was hard to grasp. My mind was awash with images and sensations. Omaha and Utah beaches. [The battles at] Avranches. St. Lo. Mortain. Argentan-Falaise. Bastogne. St. Vith. Aachen. The Roer dams. Metz. Cologne. Remagen. Across that large, blood-drenched swath of Europe, 586,628 American soldiers had fallen—135,576 to rise no more. The grim figures haunted me. I could hear the cries of the wounded, smell the stench of death. I could not sleep; I closed my eyes and thanked God for victory."

Eisenhower evaluated both Bradley and Patton after the war. In Stephen Ambrose's biography, *Eisenhower,* Ike is quoted as saying:

> *Of all the ground commanders I have known, ever, and of those of whom I've read, I would put Omar Bradley in the highest classification. In every aspect of military command, from the planning of an operation to the cleanup after its success, Brad was outstanding. I have yet to meet his equal as an offensive leader and a defensive bulwark, as a wielder of every arm that can be practically employed against an enemy.*
>
> *Patton was a master of fast and overwhelming pursuit. Headstrong by nature, and fearlessly aggressive, Patton was the more colorful figure of the two, compelling attention by his mannerisms as much as by his deeds. Bradley, however, was a master of every military maneuver, lacking only the capacity—possibly the willingness—to dramatize himself. This, I think, is to his credit.*

After the war, Bradley was appointed administrator of veterans affairs in Washington, becoming "supreme big brother" to veterans and their dependents. He supervised the medical care of 100,000 hospitalized servicemen and approved disability payments for more than two million others. He also put together programs for the rehabilitation, training, and schooling of veterans under the GI Bill, a government program to assist returned servicemen.

Two years later Bradley succeeded Eisenhower as chief of staff, and in August 1949 was sworn in as the first chairman of the Joint Chiefs of Staff. He served until 1953, then retired to become a business executive for the Bulova Watch Company and several other corporations.

In 1950, Bradley had been appointed to the rank of five-star general, sharing the highest military rank with Eisenhower, George C. Marshall, Henry "Hap" Arnold, and Douglas MacArthur. He also became the first chairman of the military committee of NATO.

Lt. Gen. Omar N. Bradley (right), commander of the 12th Army, with Lt. Gen. George S. Patton (left), commanding general of the Third Army, and General Dwight D. Eisenhower (center) at a tour of the front during World War II.
(U.S. Army Military History Institute)

Bradley did not see active duty in the Korean War, though he was there twice during the fighting. He did, however, join with General Eisenhower and others in helping plan strategy and advising General Douglas MacArthur and President Harry S Truman on the war.

Bradley retired from full-time government service in 1953, and he and his wife moved to Southern California where he enjoyed hunting, fishing, golf, and skeet shooting. The Bradleys' daughter, Elizabeth (Lee), married Henry (Hal) Beukema, an Air Force pilot. They had four children before he was killed at the age of 29 when his F-86 jet fighter crashed in the James River near Langley, Virginia, in 1954. In 1957, the Bradleys moved back to Washington, D.C., to be near their daughter and grandchildren.

Bradley's wife Mary died in 1965, and he later married Kitty Buhler, a screenwriter.

Omar Bradley died of a blood clot in the brain on April 8, 1981, in New York City at the age of 88. He was buried with full military honors at Arlington National Cemetery. He was the last surviving five-star American general of World War II.

Chronology

February 12, 1893	born in Clark, Missouri
1915	graduates from West Point; commissioned a 2nd lieutenant
1936	teaches tactics at West Point
1937	plans and training officer at West Point
1938	assistant secretary on War Department General Staff
1941	commandant of Infantry School, Fort Benning, Georgia; becomes a brigadier general
1942	promoted to major general; becomes commanding general of 82nd Infantry Division, then of 28th Infantry Division
1943	field aide to General Eisenhower in North Africa; commands U.S. Second Army and captures Bizerte and Tunis in Tunisia; causes German surrender of 40,000 soldiers; leads successful invasion of Sicily; called to England to confer on Normandy invasion
1944	commands invasion forces ashore on D-Day, June 6; commands 12th Army Corps in pushing Germans back in France
1945	leads GIs in smashing through the Siegfried Line to cross the Rhine and overrun western Germany;

	after war, appointed administrator of veterans affairs
1947	succeeds Eisenhower as chief of staff; becomes first chairman of Joint Chiefs of Staff
1953	retires to become businessman
April 8, 1981	dies in New York City; buried in Arlington National Cemetery

Further Reading

Books by Omar Bradley
Bradley: A Soldier's Story. New York: Henry Holt, 1951. Detailed narrative of his life and career, with photos and maps.

A General's Life. New York: Simon & Schuster, 1983. Extensive autobiography written with Clay Blair, covering World War II and Korean War.

Books About Omar Bradley
Ambrose, Stephen E. *Eisenhower.* New York: Simon & Schuster, 1983. Frequent references to Bradley's career.

Army Times. *Famous American Military Leaders of World War II.* New York: Dodd, Mead, 1962. Short biography of the general by the *Army Times* staff.

Article About Omar Bradley
Current Biography, 1943. New York: H.W. Wilson, 1943. Biography of Bradley up to 1943.

Captain Curtis E. LeMay (1906–1990) Army Air Corps Commander in Europe and the Pacific

Gen. Curtis E. LeMay.
(Courtesy of the Smithsonian Institution)

By his own account, Curtis LeMay was four years old when he saw his first airplane, in the sky over his home in Columbus, Ohio, in 1910. It had come from nowhere and he wanted to catch it. He thought it would be wonderful to have it for himself.

When he couldn't reach up and get the amazing flying-machine, he went home in tears. The thought then came to him:

Some day, when he was old and big enough, he would fly an airplane.

And fly he did. Thirty-two years later, as Captain Curtis E. LeMay, he would lead a squadron of B-17 Flying Fortresses in the skies over Germany in some of the most vicious air battles in history. He became a pioneer in the concept of strategic bombardment, devising some of the most innovative aerial strategies of World War II, including low-level B-29 bombings that devastated Japan. In *Iron Eagle*, Thomas Coffey says, it was said that "LeMay was to the bomber what [General George S.] Patton was to the tank."

After the war, LeMay commanded American air forces in the 1948 Berlin Airlift, which prevented the Soviet Union from taking over postwar Berlin. He then developed the Strategic Air Command, America's first line of air defense and deterrence against nuclear attack.

Curtis Emerson LeMay was born on November 15, 1906, in Columbus, Ohio, the son of a steelworker. Attending public schools there, he was a quiet, good student. He sold newspapers after school and on weekends, and spent his leisure time building crystal "wireless" radios or hunting with gun and bowie knife in the hills of southern Ohio.

After high school, his ambition was to go to the U.S. Military Academy at West Point, but he could not get the necessary appointment from his congressman. Instead, he enrolled in the School of Engineering at Ohio State University and joined the Reserve Officers' Training Corps. He paid his way through college working the overnight shift at an iron foundry and was graduated in 1928.

The year before, a daring young American pilot named Charles A. Lindbergh had excited the world by being the first to fly a plane solo across the Atlantic from the United States to Paris, France. Curtis LeMay, like many other young men, decided to become a pilot. He enlisted in the regular army and, after a year of flight training, was commissioned a 2nd lieutenant in the Army Air Corps in 1930, assigned to the 27th Pursuit Squadron at Selfridge Field, Michigan.

Over the next few years, LeMay became an expert pilot, flying in planes with open cockpits and taking part in air shows that tested the capabilities and endurance of the latest planes.

After completing advanced flight training at the Aerial Navigator School at Langley Field, Virginia, in 1934, he became one of the Air Corps' first aerial navigators. That same year he married Helen Maitland, a registered nurse.

LeMay was promoted to 1st lieutenant in 1935, and two years later served as operations and intelligence officer of the 49th Bombardment Squadron at Langley, becoming one of the first navigator-pilots to fly the new B-17 heavy bomber. The B-17s were nicknamed "Flying Fortresses" because they were so big, they looked like forts with wings. While he was on duty in Virginia, a daughter, Patricia June, was born to the LeMays.

LeMay piloted one of a group of B-17s on a training test mission from Langley to the West Coast, then on a much longer test to South America early in 1938. On that mission, LeMay came to a realization that made a lasting impact on his life and work. He put it this way in his autobiography, *Mission With LeMay—My Story:*

> *It is sad that all people of the world cannot know all other people in the world. If they could, it would simplify a lot of things. Man's affectionate sympathy ought to extend to all nationalities; but it doesn't. It just extends to the ones he knows, or feels that he understands—the ones which he can reconstruct personally in image when they're absent. That's unless the man is a god. Not many gods around.*

LeMay didn't look like a man with such a sensitive nature. He was broadchested and stocky, with a wide jaw and piercing eyes. He seldom smiled, looked fearsome, and was most always chewing or smoking cigars. Under his tough exterior was a warm, good man who was devoted to his family, friends, and the men who soon would fight under him.

LeMay then led three of the bombers on a "blind" navigational mission 700 miles out over the Atlantic Ocean in foggy weather, with a compass and little else to guide him, and successfully found his "target," the *Rex*, an Italian cruise ship. No one would say so officially, but LeMay and his fellow pilots knew that all the test flights were to prepare them and the B-17s for war.

LeMay was promoted to captain in 1940 and was assigned to the 41st Reconnaissance Squadron at Langley Field as operations and intelligence officer. The following January, he became commander of the 7th Bombardment Squadron and then group operations officer at Westover Field in Massachusetts.

Early in the spring of 1941, LeMay's expert navigational skills led to him being assigned to map aerial routes across the North Atlantic Ocean to England and over the South Atlantic to Africa, which soon would be used to ferry planes to those destinations. LeMay loved the mission. Now he was flying B-17s all over the world.

He was promoted to major that March, selected because of his extensive experience in long-range, over-water navigation and because of his pioneering work in establishing the ferrying routes.

When World War II began, LeMay was promoted to colonel, and in March 1942 was assigned to create and command the 305th Bombardment Group. To prepare for bombing missions over Europe, LeMay and his pilots flew their B-17s night and day on training flights at Muroc Dry Lake, California (later named Edwards Air Force Base). He didn't have enough planes or men for the job given him, so he worked those he had very hard.

"At least I had my own whip cracking about my own ears and ankles," LeMay wrote later in his autobiography. "This was *my* outfit. This was what I was going to take to the war and fight with."

It was around this time that LeMay picked up a nickname that is best described in his own words:

"It was in those days that I won my vulgar nickname: Iron Ass. Newspapers and magazines would try to soften it up through the years; they called me Iron Pants. This was my natural reward for working everybody as hard as I did, all personnel included."

That fall, while preparing to take his unit to England, he learned from a physical examination that he had Bell's palsy, a paralysis in the nerves of the right side of his face. It had been caused by an infection from a virus he caught while run-down from working about 20 hours a day. The facial paralysis never completely left LeMay, and doubtless caused his stern look and resulted in the rumor that he never smiled. The right side of his face couldn't.

LeMay took his unit to England where it became part of the Eighth Air Force Bomber Command and one of the first U.S. bombardment units to enter combat in World War II.

After a few bombing missions over Nazi-occupied France and Germany, LeMay began to realize that few American bombs were hitting their targets. While investigating the problem, he was told that penetrating the Luftwaffe's fighter defenses was very difficult or that enemy aircraft fire was very heavy at the target sites. In order for the Allies' planes to return safely in the daylight raids, they had to evade the enemy's gunfire.

LeMay knew what the solution was. He ordered that there would be "no more evasive action on the final bombing run," even during the heaviest enemy gunfire. The planes would stay on course, bomb their targets, and take even the most severe flak. LeMay put his own life on the line by leading the first strike to employ the new tactic. On November 23, 1942, the 305th attacked Nazi submarine pens at the German-held French Atlantic port of St. Nazaire.

The mission was a success and, afterward, all LeMay's men flew an 18-plane "box" formation in a straight line over a target. When one plane was hit or had engine trouble and had to drop out or was shot down, another would move up to take its place. The unique formation gave the squadron the maximum concentration of firepower against enemy planes attacking from any angle.

LeMay and his men were put to their most extreme test in August 1943 when the 8th Air Force began large-scale raids on targets deep in Germany's industrial heartland. Their first assignment: Bomb the factories at Regensburg where one-third of the infamous Messerschmitt fighter planes were produced.

LeMay ordered his pilots again to stay on course, no matter what the level of enemy resistance. Coffey says in *Iron Eagle*, LeMay told them: "If some of us get killed, it's too damned bad!" His men were all young, in their twenties, and he was 36, one of the youngest air commanders in the war. What followed was one of the greatest air battles of the war. LeMay lost 24 of his 127 planes, but the enemy's aircraft factories were blown to bits. His gunners had shot down at least 60 enemy planes. It was a costly victory, but LeMay's courage under fire was rewarded with America's second highest decoration, the Distinguished Service Medal.

In August 1943, LeMay devised a new "shuttle" strategy for bombing missions that greatly increased the survival rate of his pilots. On many long flights, his planes would run out of gas after hitting their targets and couldn't get back to England. LeMay told his pilots to hit their targets, then fly on instead to North African airfields.

Soon his successful formation, bombing, and retreat tactics were adopted by air units throughout the entire European Allied command. LeMay was promoted to major general. At the age of 37, he became one of the youngest officers in the U.S. Army to attain that rank. Then he took part in the first big bombing raid against Berlin in which 660 bombers struck Germany's largest city.

LeMay continued with the 8th Air Force in England as commanding general of the Third Bombardment Division through June 1944. He was awarded another Distinguished Service Medal for his work in England.

LeMay's services were then needed in the Pacific. He was reassigned to China in August 1944, to take charge of the 20th Bomber Command fighting in the China-Burma-India theater of operations. Under LeMay, China-based B-29 Superfortresses made three attacks on Japanese-held Manchurian industrial centers in July and August.

LeMay also took leadership of the 21st Bomber Command to make air strikes on the Japanese mainland. In January 1945, he made the decision to attempt low-level night attacks on Tokyo, dropping incendiary bombs that would set the city on fire. His planes would take off from Guam and other bases that recently had been regained. The night raids would make it a little easier to avoid Japanese antiaircraft batteries over the city, which could take down more of his planes if they flew in daylight.

Fire-bombing Tokyo had not been an easy decision for LeMay to make. Thousands of civilians would be killed, but Japanese industry had to be destroyed, and he hoped it would shorten the war. If Japan was not bombed into submission, an invasion would cost many American lives, perhaps a million.

The Americans under LeMay's command took the Japanese by surprise this time, in what became known as the Tokyo "fire raid" of March 9, 1945. New B-29 Superfortresses were used, and gunners and ammunition were not taken aboard, so the planes could carry more bombs. Deadly M-69 incendiary bombs were dropped *en masse*. Each bomb exploded at 2,000 feet, raining down 38 balls of liquid fire. At least 15 square miles of the industrial heart of the world's largest city were destroyed. The raid on Tokyo was called the greatest single disaster inflicted on an enemy in military history up to that time.

LeMay and his airmen followed the Tokyo "fire-raid" with similar attacks on Nagoya, Osaka, and Kobe, sometimes using as many as 500 bombers.

On August 1, 1945, LeMay ended his command of the B-29s in the Pacific to become chief of staff to General Carl Spaatz of the U.S. Strategic Air Forces, becoming second in command and in charge of all other officers in the unit. Now he took a major part in planning the atomic bombing of Hiroshima and Nagasaki.

The Japanese had been hit hard and often, causing great damage. But LeMay and other American military leaders had thought the enemy could be beaten with major air strikes followed by a costly land invasion of Japan itself, even if this meant that thousands of American soldiers and Marines would probably die.

There was an alternative, though a drastic one. American scentists had successfully tested an atomic bomb near Alamogordo, New Mexico, on July 16, 1945. The test was the culmination of a huge and secret program of U.S. scientific research and technological development, which had begun in 1940, to develop a weapon deriving its explosive force from the release of atomic energy through the fission (splitting) of heavy nuclei.

American military leaders conferred in secret on whether to drop an atomic bomb on Japan and cause such great damage of life and property that the Japanese would surrender. LeMay and other high-level officers preferred that the atomic bomb not be used to end the war because they did not think it was necessary.

On August 6, 1945, an atomic bomb was dropped on Hiroshima, with an estimated equivalent explosive force of 20,000 tons of TNT. The blast was followed three days later by a second, more powerful bomb dropped on Nagasaki. Both caused widespread death, injury, and destruction.

Japan announced its surrender on August 14, and formally signed a treaty of peace aboard the battleship U.S.S. *Missouri* on September 2.

In *Iron Eagle,* Coffey says President Harry S Truman later wrote that

> *The final decision of where and when to use the atomic bomb was up to me. Let there be no mistake about it. I regarded the bomb as a military weapon and never had any doubt that it should be used. The top military advisers to the President recommended its use,*

and when I talked to [British Prime Minister Winston] Churchill, he unhesitatingly told me he favored the use of the atomic bomb if it might aid to end the war.

Twenty years later, LeMay wrote in his autobiography, "I did not and do not decry the use of the bomb. Anything which will achieve the desired results should be employed. If those bombs shortened the war only by days, they rendered an inestimable service, and so did the men who were responsible for their construction and delivery."

LeMay was in attendance for the surrender ceremonies in Tokyo Bay. He wrote about it in his autobiography:

Wish I could recall exactly what went through my mind while standing on that open deck of the Missouri. I did think of the young men who died to bring about this moment of triumph and, as always, wondered just where I'd gone wrong in losing as many as we did. Seemed to me that if I had done a better job we might have saved a few more crews.

Our ears were filled with the roar of four hundred and sixty-two B-29s flying overhead. They came from every wing, every group, every squadron.

Thomas Coffey says in *Iron Eagle—The Turbulent Life of Curtis LeMay* that LeMay's superiors gave him the highest praise for the part he played in fighting the war. The day before the atomic bombing of Hiroshima, General Spaatz telegraphed Lauris Norstad, then chief of staff for the 20th Air Force, about LeMay and his command: "HAVE HAD OPPORTUNITY TO CHECK UP ON BAKER TWO NINE OPERATIONS AND BELIEVE THIS IS THE BEST ORGANIZED AND MOST TECHNICALLY AND TACTICALLY PROFICIENT MILITARY ORGANIZATION THAT THE WORLD HAS SEEN TO DATE."

LeMay thought he had done more than his best. He wrote later, "Considering the problems we faced [in the air war against Japan], I think we did a hell of a job. We got it done."

After some farewells to friends on Guam, he flew a B-29 Superfort on a record-breaking nonstop flight from Japan to

Chicago and was rewarded with a hero's welcome upon his return. Then he went home to Ohio.

LeMay was urged to run for the U.S. Senate, but declined, saying he wanted to stay in the Army Air Corps. He served as

Gen. Curtis E. LeMay (right), commanding general of the Strategic Air Command in 1948, confers with Gen. George Kenney.
(Courtesy National Air and Space Museum, Smithsonian Institution)

first deputy chief of air staff for research and development and helped organize satellite and missile programs.

In 1947, the U.S. Air Force became a separate branch of the military service. LeMay was appointed its European commander, with headquarters at Wiesbaden, West Germany. The following June, the Soviets cut off Allied access to West Berlin, and LeMay was put in charge of the "Berlin Airlift," flying food and other essential supplies to the blockaded city. It became one of the most dramatic events of the Cold War.

In October 1948, LeMay became commanding general of the Strategic Air Command, which coordinated U.S. air defenses for possible alerts anywhere in the world. He was promoted to vice chief of staff of the air force in 1957 and served as chief of staff from 1961 until his retirement in 1965.

LeMay won numerous American and foreign awards for his leadership and heroism, including the Medal for Humane Action for personally flying many of the Berlin Airlift missions. He ran unsuccessfully for vice president of the United States with independent presidential candidate George Wallace in 1968.

He advocated all means to end the war in Vietnam, even the use of nuclear weapons. But he did not say what was mistakenly attributed to him about the war, and which turned many people against him. He never suggested that Vietnam be bombed back into the Stone Age. LeMay's biographer, Mac-Kinlay Kantor, put those words in his mouth, and LeMay had not proofread the manuscript closely enough to discover the fiction before the book was published. It caused a storm of unfair controversy, which LeMay was never able to completely put behind him. Despite that, he is remembered today as one of the most important and celebrated heroes of World War II.

Coffey said of him in *Iron Eagle:*

In World War II he was so daring, ingenious, and effective, first against the Germans and then the Japanese, that he became America's most famous air commander—in the minds of most experts the greatest this country has ever produced.

Curtis E. LeMay personally led his Flying Fortresses across fiercely defended German skies in some of the most vicious air battles of all time. He had about him the same aura of unflinching toughness as [General George S.] Patton.

He devised some of the most innovative aerial strategies of the Second World War, including the low-level B-29 attacks that devastated Japan.

A few hours before LeMay's retirement on February 1, 1965, President Lyndon B. Johnson presented him with his fourth Distinguished Service Medal.

In retirement, LeMay resumed his boyhood interest in hunting, took up amateur radio broadcasting, and added a new hobby, building sports cars. Curtis LeMay died October 1, 1990, in the hospital at March Air Force Base in Riverside, California.

Chronology

November 15, 1906	born in Columbus, Ohio
1928	graduated from Ohio State University School of Engineering
1929	enlists in regular army
1930	commissioned 2nd lieutenant in Army Air Corps
1934	becomes aerial navigator and marries Helen Maitland
1935	commissioned 1st lieutenant
1937–38	flies B-17s with 49th Bombardment Squadron
1940	promoted to captain
1941	maps aerial routes to England and South America; promoted to major, then colonel
1942	commands 305th Bombardment Group in England; bombs Nazi Europe
1943	bombs Regensburg, Germany; devises "shuttle" bombing strategy
1944	commands 20th Bomber Command in Pacific
1945	leads 21st Bomber Command in "fire-raids" on Tokyo; becomes chief of staff of U.S. Strategic Air Forces; witnesses Japanese surrender
1947	commands U.S. Air Forces in Europe

1948	takes charge of "Berlin Airlift"; becomes commanding general of Strategic Air Command
1957	promoted to Air Force vice chief of staff
1961–65	serves as Air Force chief of staff
1965	retires
1968	runs unsuccessfully for vice president
October 1, 1990	dies in Riverside, California

Further Reading

Book by Curtis E. LeMay
Mission With LeMay—My Story. Garden City, N.Y.: Doubleday, 1965. Autobiography written with MacKinlay Kantor; a detailed analysis of LeMay's military career.

Books About Curtis E. LeMay
Anders, Curtis. *Fighting Airmen.* New York: Putnam, 1966. Short biographies of LeMay and other American air leaders.

Coffey, Thomas M. *Iron Eagle—The Turbulent Life of General Curtis LeMay.* New York: Crown, 1986. A thorough biography by a noted military historian.

Craven, W.E., and Cate, J.L. *The Army Air Forces in World War II.* Chicago: University of Chicago Press, 1948. Summary of LeMay's air force career in the war.

General George S. Patton Jr. (1885–1945) Commander, 2nd Armored Division and Third Army

General George S. Patton Jr., commanding general of U.S. Third Army, in 1945.
(U.S. Army Military History Institute)

General Dwight D. Eisenhower, commander of the Allied forces in the D-Day invasion of Normandy on June 6, 1944, was far from satisfied with the Americans' meager 30-mile advance into France in the month after the landing. The German Army was holding firm, and he needed a military leader who could push the offensive forward and drive the Germans back out of France, no matter how hard the fighting or what the cost in manpower.

The best man for the job was George S. Patton Jr., a tank commander who had already proven his ability to win over tremendous odds with his victories in Morocco and Sicily. But he was in disgrace over having slapped a soldier under his command, and high officials demanded Patton be court-martialed. The soldier had been hospitalized for a bad case of war nerves, but Patton had considered him a coward and slapped his face.

Eisenhower reprimanded Patton and relieved him of his command, but could not waste the talents of one of the best fighting leaders he had. Instead of court-martialing Patton, Ike promoted him to the rank of major general, put him in charge of the Third Army, and assigned him to spearhead the Allied drive through France and into Germany.

"No operation better suited Patton's special qualifications than the break-through," says Harry H. Semmes in his biography, *Portrait of Patton*. "In it his audacity, speed and tactical skill all became at once manifest, for an operation of this type was ideal for a bold armored leader."

Patton was given an untried army, freshly arrived from training in the United States. He looked like no general the green soldiers had ever seen, in riding pants and tight-fitting battle jacket with rows of ribbons for valor on his chest, his boots glistening and their spurs flashing as he carried a riding crop.

Semmes says Patton pushed the troops hard in training until, as one soldier later said, "You felt that here was a man you would go to hell and back for." "Now," Patton told his men, "let's get the hell on to Berlin."

Semmes says that he was considered the greatest combat general of modern times. "[He was] hot-tempered and profane, but at the same time, humble before God, sentimental and deeply profound in his way of life, whose leadership permeated armored and mobile warfare, and all those he commanded."

The battles Patton and the Third Army fought in the months after the Normandy invasion were some of the greatest not only of the war, but also in American military history. Their victories were major factors in the Allies' eventual defeat of the Germans.

George Smith Patton Jr. was born November 11, 1885, in San Gabriel, California. His grandfather, a colonel in the Confederate cavalry, had been killed in the Civil War. His father had attended Virginia Military Institute but became a lawyer and businessman instead of a soldier.

When he was a boy, Patton played soldier and read books about great battles. Then, at the age of 18, he became the third generation of Pattons to enroll at Virginia Military Institute. After graduation in 1904, he went on to the U.S. Military Academy at West Point. He became a top athlete but was not a scholar, so it took him five years to graduate, and he received his commission as 2nd lieutenant in 1909.

Patton served with the 15th Cavalry at Fort Sheridan, Illinois, and began a lifelong love of horses. While at Sheridan in 1910, he married his high school sweetheart, Beatrice Ayer. Their first child, a daughter named after her mother, was born in 1911. Later the Pattons had a son and another daughter.

Patton became a member of the United States team at the 1912 Olympic games in Stockholm, Sweden, entering the modern pentathlon. He made a good show in swimming, riding, fencing, and running, but was surprisingly poor in the pistol-shooting event and finished fifth out of 30 contestants. After that, he practiced shooting every chance he got and became an expert marksman.

Patton's first taste of fighting came in 1916 when he served as aide to General John J. Pershing who commanded the "punitive expedition" in Mexico to capture the bandit chief, Pancho Villa. While on a corn-buying mission with only six soldiers, Patton learned that one of Villa's top officers was hiding nearby. He led his men in a raid on the bandit's hideout, killing General Julio Cardenas and another desperado. Pershing commended Patton and thereafter called him "Bandit."

When the United States entered World War I, Pershing named Patton to his staff, and they sailed to France in May 1917. Patton was assigned to the Tank Corps and saw action in the battle of Cambrai, when tanks were first used on a large scale by the British. Promoted to major, he commanded the 304th Brigade of the Tank Corps in two of the biggest battles of the war, the Saint-Mihiel and Meuse-Argonne offenses in northeastern France in the autumn of 1918. Wounded in the fighting, he was awarded the Distinguished Service Cross for "conspicuous courage, coolness, energy, and intelligence in directing the advance of his brigade."

By the war's end, Patton had made a name for himself in tank warfare. His peacetime duties were divided between command of tank and cavalry units until 1928, when he began a four-year stint in Washington, D.C., in the office of the chief of cavalry.

After graduation from the Army War College in 1932, Patton served with the 3rd Cavalry. Two years later he was promoted to lieutenant colonel and spent two years with the general staff in the Hawaiian Islands.

As the army stepped up its preparations for World War II, Patton was ordered to Fort Benning, Georgia, in July 1940 for duty as brigade commander with the 2nd Armored Division. The following April he was promoted to major general and became the division's commanding officer. Under Patton's leadership, the unit developed into what many called the toughest, most feared outfit in the U.S. Army.

Patton also became commander of the 1st Armored Corps and merged it with the 2nd Armored Division to organize the Desert Training Center at Indio, California. There, soldiers learned to live and fight an armored war in high temperatures and under desert conditions. Patton trained, ate, and rationed his daily water just like his men, and encouraged a spirit of camaraderie between officers and soldiers that was not found anywhere else in the army.

Patton earned a reputation as a tough military leader and boasted that tanks alone would win the war. He also became a colorful if paradoxical leader. Packing a pair of pearl-handled pistols, Patton drove himself and his men with such fury that newspaper correspondents began calling him "Old Blood and Guts." While he swore at times, which horrified chaplains, he also read the Bible every day and spent time in private prayer. Once, Semmes says, he pronounced like a preacher: "Battle is the most magnificent competition in which a human being can indulge!"

In preparation for an American invasion of North Africa, Major General Patton was placed in charge of the Western Tank Force. In November 1942, he prepared his men to land in Western Morocco by a blend of cussing, prayer, and hard training.

Patton's biographer, Harry H. Semmes, says that as the ships taking them to Africa sailed closer to Morocco, Patton sent this message to his troops: "During the first few days after you get ashore, you must work unceasingly, regardless of sleep, regardless of food. A pint of sweat will save a gallon of blood. The eyes of the world are watching us; the heart of America beats for us; God is with us. On our victory depends the freedom or slavery of the human race. We shall surely win."

Calling on God to help him lead his men into a new crusade, he won a major victory in Morocco after four days of intense fighting, from November 8 to 11. The victory came on Patton's 57th birthday.

The following March, General Eisenhower put Patton in command of the 90,000 GIs of the American II Corps in North Africa. They joined the British in an attack against the powerful German Afrika Korps' 200,000 soldiers. Semmes says Patton ordered one of his commanders: "Attack, and keep on attacking, even if you lose one-quarter of your men."

Patton always rode his jeep to the front of the lines to lead his men. During this campaign, he was promoted to lieutenant general (three stars), but wrote in his diary, "Now I want, and will get, *four* stars."

Patton and his tank corps, together with the British, all but wiped out Field Marshal Erwin Rommel's 10th Panzer (tank) Division at El Guettar, a strategically important pass in Tunisia. By April, the Afrika Korps had surrendered and Patton could claim a major victory. There had been a heavy price to pay in soldiers dead, however.

In July 1943, Eisenhower assigned Patton to command the U.S. Seventh Army in an invasion of Sicily, the island stepping-stone to Italy. It put Patton in direct competition with British Army leader General Bernard "Monty" Montgomery, who was also in Sicily by then and worked hard at getting the credit for any Allied victory he engaged in. A race began between Patton and Montgomery to take Sicily. It was a race, Patton told his troops, "We must win."

The first wave of Patton's Seventh Army landed on the beaches of Sicily on July 10, near the town of Gela. Two German divisions, led by deadly Tiger tanks, charged into the town and began pushing the Americans back toward the sea.

Offshore, American battleships shelled the town just as Patton's jeep came to a stop in front of its tallest building. Watching the battle from the top of the building, Patton saw that he and his troops in the town were cut off from those landing on the beaches. He sent a messenger to an American division outside the town with orders to link up with them inside Gela. While Nazi planes bombed the building he was using as his field headquarters, Patton received a message that the division had done as he ordered. He became so caught up in the action that day, he joined a platoon of GIs in helping take the town.

Patton's Seventh Army knifed westward to capture that half of the island while Montgomery's Eighth Army thrust north. Montgomery's task was to capture the port of Messina at the northeastern tip of the island so that the hundreds of thousands of Nazi troops on Sicily would be trapped and forced to surrender. But Patton wanted the glory that would go to the army that took Messina.

Lt. Gen. George S. Patton Jr., commander of the Seventh Army, pauses in Gela during the Sicily invasion on July 11, 1943.
(U.S. Army Military History Institute)

"This is a horse race," Semmes says Patton told one of his commanders, "in which the prestige of the U.S. Army is at stake. We must take Messina before the British."

Patton's Seventh Army captured western Sicily in 12 days and stood 150 miles west of Messina, while Montgomery's army was 100 miles south of the city. German and Italian soldiers in great numbers were rushing to Messina, hoping to escape by ship before they were trapped.

Semmes says Patton urged two other generals, Omar Bradley and Lucian Truscott, to push toward Messina, telling them, "Land your troops behind the German lines at night." When Truscott said that was too risky, Patton told him, "Be bold, be bold."

Truscott's soldiers managed to sneak ashore in the dark, and the Germans then had the Americans both in front of and behind them. As the enemy fled toward Messina, Patton and his men chased them, his advance guard entering the town on the night of August 16. The next morning, Patton and his staff drove fast for Messina while Nazi shells burst all around. One of the cars was blown off the road, but Patton kept going. He entered Messina by jeep, and only minutes later a single British tank rumbled into town carrying a general sent by Montgomery to claim Messina for him.

The British general watched as Patton stood triumphantly in the center of the town, amid cheering GIs. Semmes says the general saluted Patton and said, "It was a jolly good race, sir. I congratulate you."

Sicily was taken back from the Germans and Italians in 38 days of very heavy fighting. Afterward, military strategists said they doubted the important island could have been conquered so quickly, had it not been for Patton's driving force.

Flushed with victory, Patton then visited an evacuation hospital to cheer up the brave GIs who had been wounded in the campaign. When he saw a young soldier who had nothing visibly wrong with him, Patton asked why he was a patient. The soldier replied that his nerves were shot, and he couldn't stand the shelling anymore. While the soldier was sobbing, Patton cursed him and called him a coward. Then Patton slapped him in the face with his glove, and ordered the doctors to return the soldier to duty. The soldier had been shell-shocked from battle and hospitalized because of an emotional breakdown, but Patton did not believe in neuroses so he had no sympathy for him.

The incident was reported by one of the doctors and came to the attention of General Eisenhower. Some officers urged him to court-martial Patton, but Ike could not do without him in the war. He said Patton might sometimes be too tough on his men and talked too much, which created a very bad impression, but Eisenhower considered him to be the best fighting general he had.

Eisenhower reprimanded Patton and relieved him of his command, then sent him to England to help prepare the Third Army for the invasion of Europe. It was important duty, but Patton felt humiliated, misunderstood, and denied the chance to move his armored divisions into Berlin.

A month after the D-Day landings of the Allies in Normandy, Patton was still in England, and General Bradley was in charge of the American armies in France. Patton wrote home to his wife: "I hope they don't win the war without us. It is hell to be on the sidelines and see all the glory eluding us."

Eisenhower then returned Patton to action, promoting him to full general (four stars) and putting him in command of the Third Army, freshly arrived from the United States.

After training his troops hard, Patton now had a new companion to go into battle with. A British pilot's dog, a white bull terrier, needed a new master after his owner's death in a bombing raid over Germany. "Willie" was given to Patton and remained with him for the rest of the war.

The Allied army fought its way out of Normandy under a plan Eisenhower called Operation Cobra. On July 25, Allied planes dropped 4,200 tons of bombs in an hour and a half on German troops near the town of St. Lo in northwest France, blowing away men, tanks, and guns. A hole was finally made in the German line of defense, and Ike sent Patton and the tanks of his Third Army through it.

Patton rode in his jeep only a few miles behind his men as they pursued the Germans over the hot and dusty plains of France. Once he took personal command of a tank unit to cross a river under heavy enemy fire, clearing the way for his troops to follow.

The U.S. VII Corps then attacked west of St. Lo and made progress despite suffering 1,000 casualties. Patton led the U.S. 3rd Armored and 1st Infantry divisions in pressing ahead in two mobile columns. Meanwhile, near Caen, the British Second Army began advancing south toward the German Seventh Army's rear. Patton's easternmost column advanced under heavy German counterattacks, while to the west his second column forced its way into Coustances on July 28 and two days later reached Avranches.

Greatly outnumbered in tanks, the Germans began to lose their hold on the area when Patton's U.S. Third Army swept forward into Brittany. In desperation, on August 6, Adolph Hitler ordered five Panzer divisions to reinforce the Nazi Seventh Army, so it could mount a drive to stop the Allied advance from Normandy. But Allied land and air strikes in the battle of Mortain August 6–10 were successful in halting the Germans. On August 8, Patton turned his tanks northward through Le Mans toward Argentan, to trap the Germans in the Mortain-Falaise pocket, about 25 miles southwest of Bayeux, France, on the River Vire, as the British Second Army pressed southward. Two days later, the American VIII Corps reached Nantes on the Loire estuary. Three corps of Patton's army then began sweeping north to envelop the German Seventh Army's rear. The U.S. V Corps took Argentan on August 14, while General Henry Crerar's Canadian First Army fought south towards the Falaise Gap, where thousands of German soldiers were positioned.

In all, Patton was attacking in four directions at once, while conducting an offensive operation. This was one of the very rare instances of such action in the history of warfare.

At this time, defying Hitler's orders to keep fighting, Field Marshal Gunther von Kluge, commanding the German Army Group B, consisting of the German Seventh Army and Panzer Group West, began to withdraw his nearly trapped armies out of the Falaise pocket. After five more days, under heavy Allied air and ground assault, the Germans surrendered on August 22. About 250,000 Americans took part in the St. Lo and Falaise battles, with some 25,000 killed or injured. Of 150,000 Germans taking part, 100,000 were killed or injured and the surviving 50,000 were taken prisoner.

The road to the Seine River and Paris then lay open to the Allies. Patton and his Third Army reached Mantes-la-Jolie, 30 miles from Paris, on August 19. He could have captured the French capital in a matter of hours or, at the most, a few days, but American leaders had promised the honor of liberating Paris to others.

The U.S. First Army, commanded by General Omar Bradley, with British troops added for the occasion, together with General Jacques LeClerc's Free-French 2nd Armored Division, which had been serving under Patton, entered Paris on August 25. Patton and the Third Army, denied the glory of liberating Paris, were under orders to leave the liberation of Paris to Bradley and the French and advance eastward toward the Rhine and Berlin.

The war looked almost won in August 1944, when Patton was ordered to transfer a large number of Third Army's trucks to First Army. This impaired his ability to maintain adequate shipments of food, ammunition, and gasoline, preventing his armored divisions from advancing as fast as he wanted. His 7th Armored Division ran out of fuel 30 miles from Verdun and was ordered to retreat, but could not move in any direction, so it was hit hard by the enemy. Many other units on low gasoline supplies narrowly avoided having to suffer the same fate.

Even under these hardships, Patton's men took the French city of Nancy in mid-September, and approached the fortress city of Metz. Despite having only 400,000 gallons of gasoline on hand, slightly less than the Third Army's normal requirement for one day's operation, Patton was determined to crash through the Nazis' strongly fortified Siegfried Line along the western border of Germany and end the war.

Patton's attack began during heavy rain early in November. Despite no aerial support and heavy resistance from the Nazis, divisions from XX Corps took Metz on November 22. Meanwhile, XII Corps to the south attacked the German cities of Mainz, Frankfurt, and Darmstadt.

In December, the Germans made a surprise offensive in the Ardennes Forest in Belgium, which came to be called the Battle of the Bulge. It was a desperate gamble by Adolph Hitler to stop the Allied advance into Germany and recapture the crucial north Belgium supply port of Antwerp, on the Scheldt River.

The battle began on December 16, catching the Allies off-guard, and punched a dangerous dent or "bulge" into the American lines. Two German Panzer armies waited until severe winter weather had grounded Allied planes, then hit hard and shattered two American divisions, which cost the lives of thousands of GIs. Patton counterattacked and, though surrounded and outnumbered, saved the city of Bastogne, which deprived the Germans of capturing much-needed fuel supplies there.

The U.S. First and Ninth armies, temporarily under British Field Marshal Montgomery's command, attacked the Germans from the north, while Patton and his Third Army attacked from the south. Improved flying weather after December 24 permitted U.S. bombers to aid Allied counterattacks, and by January 15, 1945, the German forces were destroyed or routed. The Battle of the Bulge had been won at the cost of some 77,000 Allied killed or injured.

Patton kept on advancing the Third Army toward Germany and demanded that his officers never yield an inch of ground they had won. Many Germans now feared Patton more than any other American or British general. They wondered where he would strike next.

Harry Semmes writes in *Portrait of Patton* that "Patton had demonstrated his capacity for leadership throughout the campaign [the Battle of the Bulge]. His men performed many unbelievable feats of heroism that helped to turn the tide against the enemy, and Patton was more than willing to emphasize this repeatedly with praise and decorations."

In March, Patton and his men and tanks swept past German resistance and crossed the Rhine River on pontoon bridges at Oppenheim, between Mainz and Mannheim. Advancing on German soil, they joined two other Allied armies moving toward Berlin as the Soviets approached the city from the other side.

After the Allies crossed the Rhine, the American First and Ninth armies soon invaded the Ruhr industrial basin, encircling the German Army and trapping 300,000 men, two dozen generals, and an admiral.

On the way to Berlin, Patton discovered Nazi concentration camps and the horror of gas chambers at Buchenwald and Dachau. The skeleton-like prisoners he found alive were the few survivors of the millions of Jews and others who had been tortured and executed during what is now known as the Holocaust.

Soviet troops reached Berlin on April 22 and surrounded the city. Three days later, the U.S. First Army commanded by General Courtney H. Hodges and the Soviet First Ukrainian Army under Marshal Ivan Konev met at Torgau on the Elbe River, near Leipzig in east-central Germany. Hitler committed suicide in his bunker headquarters in Berlin on April 30. On May 7, his generals surrendered unconditionally at Rheims, ending the war in Europe.

After the war, Patton pleaded to be sent to fight the Japanese. Denied that, his war was over and he was flown back to the United States.

Patton was still a controversial figure, but there was no denying that in 10 months of leading the armored push through France and deep into Germany, he had earned the reputation as one of the greatest generals in American military history. His genius as an armored military strategist and tactician is recognized by military historians around the world.

Besides the vast territory Patton's Third Army had recovered, it took nearly one million prisoners, killed or wounded half a million more, and inflicted heavy damage upon the enemy's will to fight. No other U.S. army had captured so many willing prisoners.

After the war, Patton was assigned to command the Third Army occupation of the Bavarian region of Germany. He had proven his worth in war, but found himself again in hot water during the peace. Critical of postwar American foreign policy, he outraged politicians by declaring that America would have to fight the Soviet Union sooner or later, so why not now?

Patton was again reprimanded and stripped of his command. He returned to the United States and found the nation divided on whether he was a hero or a dangerous egomaniac.

He was soon ordered back to Germany to assume peacetime command of the Fifteenth Army and was glad to be away from politicians and reporters, back with his men, tanks, and horses.

On December 9, 1945, Patton was riding in his limousine on the way to shoot pheasants with a friend when, on a narrow road near Mannheim, his car was hit by an approaching army truck that veered into his lane. In the collision, Patton's head hit the ceiling of the car, and his neck and spinal cord were severely injured. He lived another 12 days, at a hospital in nearby Heidelberg, then died on December 21.

Chronology

___

November 11, 1885	born in San Gabriel, California
1903	enters Virginia Military Institute
1909	graduates from West Point; commissioned a second lieutenant; appointed to 15th Cavalry at Fort Sheridan, Illinois
1910	marries Beatrice Banning Ayer
1912	competes in Pentathlon at Olympic Games in Stockholm, Sweden
1916	joins expeditionary force in Mexico
1917	promoted to captain; organizes a tank unit in France in World War I
1918	promoted to major and then lieutenant colonel; active in Saint-Mihiel and Meuse-Argonne offensives; promoted to colonel
1920	joins 3rd Cavalry at Fort Myer, Va., as commanding officer
1924	graduates from Command and General Staff College
1928	joins office of the chief of cavalry in in Washington, D.C.
1938	takes command of 1st Cavalry Division
1940	becomes commanding officer of 2nd Armored Brigade at Fort Benning, Georgia; promoted to brigadier general

1941	promoted to major general; becomes commander of 2nd Armored Division
1942	commands 1st Armored Corps in North Africa; victorious in Morocco
1943	commands Seventh Army in victory in Sicily; beats the British to Messina; promoted to lieutenant general; slaps soldier and is relieved of command
1944	commands Third Army in Europe
1945	promoted to full general and given command of Third Army occupation force in Bavaria
December 21, 1945	dies in Heidelberg from auto accident

Further Reading

Books About George S. Patton

Army Times, editors. *Warrior: The Story of General George S. Patton, Jr.* New York: Putnam, 1967. Fast-moving, very readable biography for adults or young adults.

Devaney, John. *"Blood and Guts," The True Story of Gen. George S. Patton, USA.* New York: Messner, 1982. Good general biography for young adults.

Farago, Ladislas. *Patton: Ordeal and Triumph.* New York: Obolensky, 1963. Complete, comprehensive biography for adult readers.

Peifer, Charles, Jr. *Soldier of Destiny, a Biography of George Patton.* Minneapolis: Dillon Press, 1989. Easy-to-read, fast paced biography for teenagers.

Semmes, Harry H. *Portrait of Patton.* New York: Appleton-Century-Crofts, 1955. An informative, well-written biography for adults or young adults.

Index

Boldface headings indicate extensive treatment of a topic.
Italic locators indicate illustrations and captions.

Index

Index

Index

Index

Index